Lessons From
The Big House

One Family's Passage Through
The History Of The South

A Memoir

Frye Gaillard

Researched with Nancy B. Gaillard

Down Home Press, Asheboro, N.C.

ISBN 1-878086-31-6

Library of Congress Number 94-067915

Printed in the United States of America

Cover Design by Ginger F. Harris
Book Design by Mason R. Harris

94 95 96 97 98 99 10 9 8 7 6 5 4 3 2 1

Down Home Press
P.O. Box 4126
Asheboro, N.C. 27204

This book is a graduation present to my daughters, Rachel and Tracy Gaillard, who have expressed an interest from time to time in who they are and where they came from, and in the troubled, heroic history of the South.

TABLE OF CONTENTS

Palmer Gaillard at 95

Introduction

The old man had a certain presence about him, and he still lives for me in scattered pieces of memory — the wispy white hair and piercing eyes, and the frailties that slowly whittled away at his vigor. I remember the morning of his 100th birthday. I had spent a few minutes picking flowers for him — a handful of bridal wreath and azaleas, a sprig of wisteria that was beginning to droop. All in all, it was a puny bouquet alongside the others, which came from the best-connected people in the state. The old man had become an institution of sorts — the acknowledged dean of the Alabama bar. He was still trying cases in his 98th year, no doubt the oldest lawyer in the country, and some people said he was one of the best.

I didn't know about that. I was nine-years-old when he turned 100, and as his youngest grandson, the thing I liked about him was his stories. The Civil War had ended when he was not quite 10, and he was full of tales about the last days of it — Yankee soldiers marching toward the house, his mother defiant, her servants rushing to hide the silver in the woods. He took me up to the attic one time, a musty alcove in his antebellum house where portraits of the ancestors stared from the walls. He found an old trunk with a battered lock, and opened it carefully. A Confederate uniform lay inside, gray with parallel rows of brass buttons on the chest. There was a ragged hole near one of the buttons — the work of moths, my grandfather said, though I told my friends when I showed it to them later that this was the place where the bullet had struck.

It was, I suppose, a curious way to grow up, surrounded by the relics and the old man's stories. But that realization didn't dawn until later, nor did I see, until I was well past the years of my own adolescence, that my grandfather was more than a teller of tales. He was obsessed by the larger meaning of the past, that delicate body of knowledge and understanding that each generation passes to the next.

He called me aside on his 100th birthday, and my memory of the moment is as vivid as if it had happened yesterday. He was dressed as usual in his pin striped suit, charcoal gray, with a vest and carefully knotted tie, and he was sitting in a rocker on the Big House porch. The view from that particular veranda was nice. It was March 26, the peak of spring in Mobile, Alabama, with the dogwoods blooming, the Spanish moss streaming from the live oak trees, and the fronds beginning to turn green on the palms. The old man smiled as I sat down beside him. He thanked me for the flowers I had picked for his birthday, and then he gave me a book. It was a slender volume with a plain brown cover — 33 pages of family genealogy that he had put together in the preceding summer. Inside the cover, he had written me a note, the handwriting wobbly, the lines drifting slowly toward the top of the page.

> My dear grandson, I am presenting you this history of your Gaillard ancestors... They have set us a very high standard for living and we should try to carry it on unsullied. Your loving grandfather, S.P. Gaillard

At the age of nine, I wasn't quite sure that I understood, but later I knew that the book and the note both were an expression of the old man's passion. He had become the self-appointed keeper of the family myth, the whisper of the ancestors drifting through the years, giving testament to the notion of the European romantics that the dead simply go to live in our hearts. And yet I also knew, despite my grandfather's reverence, that it was a difficult legacy he was seeking to impart — full of flaws and complications — and there was a time in my life when I simply dismissed it. I came of age in the 1960s, when the South was coming to terms with its past. It was not very pretty. Whatever the strengths in the Southern way of life, it was tainted by a history of slavery and segregation. For nearly 300 years, my family had been a part of that taint, amassing slaves by the end of the 17th century, and supporting white supremacy well into the 20th. At least for me in the 1960s, none of that seemed to be a cause for much pride.

And yet somehow the old voices lingered, and 30 years after my grandfather's death, I found myself searching through the things in his attic. The last of his children — two daughters and a son who had lived until their 80s — had finally died, leaving the Big House cluttered with reminders. There were old books and clothes and furniture that came from the 18th century, and there was also a cardboard box in the attic, nestled against the side of an antique chest. Inside was a copy of the old man's book — the family genealogy tucked away with some letters and other relics from the past.

I took the box with me, and though I ignored it for the next several months, eventually I began to sift through the contents. The deeper I dug, the clearer it became that a story had been buried away in these papers. It was an ordinary story in many ways — one family's passage through the history of the South, producing no George Washingtons or Robert E. Lees. And yet there it was, tracing back to the wars of the 17th century, when thousands of French protestants, including the Gaillards, were forced to flee their country to survive. Some of them came to the American colonies, and they left a trail of paper along the way — deeds and letters and certificates of baptism — thin at first with only a handful of names, dates and places. But at least by the time of the American Revolution, real people had begun to emerge from the mists — characters that I could begin to see and understand, and the most remarkable thing about them was this: They spoke in a language that I knew very well.

I could hear my grandfather's voice in theirs, and even my own was shaped in part by a character that emerged over 12 generations. This is the story of how that happened — of one Southern family and the history that surrounds it. It's a story that begins in the south of France, with the ambitions of a king and the terror of the people who were caught in his way....

Part I
Survival

Chapter 1
The First Generations

They came from the land of Languedoc, famous for its wines and its tradition of heresy. The land rose quickly from the Mediterranean Sea, the swamps giving way to rocky hillsides and the Pyrenees Mountains rising in the west. Six miles from the sea was Montpelier, a medium-sized city on the trading roads of Europe, where the Roman Way passed on its route to Paris.

On July 19, 1625, Joachim Gaillard was born in that city, the son of Jean Gaillard and his wife Marie, who gave him the Spanish name of his grandfather. As the family gathered for the baby's baptism — the parents, a cousin, the maternal grandfather — you had to imagine there was hope in their hearts, stirred inevitably by the gift of new life. But they also knew these were perilous times, with holy wars looming in the French countryside. Eight years earlier, in 1616, a cousin had been tortured and killed on the rack, a gift from the Romans to the inquisitions of Europe. In the family retelling of the story he was brave, more certain of his faith with every turn of the crank — and yet they could also hear his screams, as his tendons and ligaments were beginning to tear, and his body, quite literally, was pulled into pieces.

It wasn't supposed to be this way. On April 13, 1598, King Henry IV signed a proclamation at the city of Nantes, granting civil rights and full freedom of religion to the protestant minority in the south of France. But Henry was murdered in 1610, and the position of the Protestants, or Huguenots as they were then known, began to deteriorate in a hurry. King Louis XIV was determined to consolidate the power of the throne, and a cornerstone of his growing ambition was a national identity based partly on religion. On October 18, 1685, after decades of strife, he decided to revoke the Edict of Nantes, and with it the rights of the French Huguenots.

They began to flee the country after that. Many went to Prussia, where their thrift and middle class skills were welcomed, but a substantial minority boarded ships for America. One of those was Joachim Gaillard, now in his 60s, who left France with his wife and three grown sons. Nothing is known of their voyage to America, though it probably came early in 1687, in an effort to avoid the hurricane season. A bad one had hit in the preceding fall, doing great damage to the village of Charleston, which was the place where the Gaillards got off the boat.

Charles Town, as it was known at its founding, wasn't much to see in the 1680s — a frontier town with wooden buildings and quagmire streets and a population that had recently risen to 1,000. But there was also something exciting about it, for it was a melting pot of European refugees — the British and French, Scotch-Irish and Dutch, even a few Sephardic Jews from the southern tip of Portugal. They were drawn in part by the promise of freedom, a constitution written by the philosopher, John Locke, and they were carried also by the Atlantic trade winds, which blew from the Azores to the West Indies, then northward to brush against the Carolina coast — making Charleston the most promising port in the South.

On October 10, 1687, Joachim and his sons bought their first piece of land — a grant of 600 acres at the price of 30 pounds. It was a tract in the swamps along the Santee River, 35 miles from Charleston by land, or nearly 100 if you followed the rivers by canoe. They found some stone on a high piece of ground and used it to build the foundation of the house, for that was the way they had done it in France. The original structure no longer survives, but the English explorer, John Lawson, marveled when he saw it in 1701. "A very curious contriv'd House built of Brick and Stone," he wrote in his journal on January 12.

It was 4 p.m., a wet winter Sunday, when Lawson and his party first came upon the house. They had crossed the murky waters of Wambaw Creek, flanked by cypress and some palmetto shrubs, and after a day of paddling against the Santee current, it was time to stop. Night was falling and the mosquitos were out, even though the weather was bitterly cold. Lawson had never seen anything like it, and he was grateful for a night at the Gaillard place. But the next morning he was gone, heading for the rice plantation of Joachim's oldest son, Bartholomew Gaillard, which was the last white dwelling in the Santee basin.

By the middle of the day, the explorers were lost. The woods were flooded from the heavy winter rains, and with most of the familiar landmarks submerged, even Lawson's Indian guide was baffled. After a brief consultation with his six-member party, Lawson sent the Indian and three others to explore, while the rest of them waited on a patch of higher ground. Six hours later, the Indian returned, barely able to paddle because he was drunk.

"This assur'd us," Lawson wrote in his journal, "they had found some Place of Refreshment."

The place, he discovered, was Bartholomew's house, where the Frenchmen were celebrating with their guests. "A very kind, loving and affable people," Lawson wrote, but he appreciated more than the French hospitality, or their bracing rum drinks on a cold winter's day. They were carving a home from the Low Country swamps, enduring the hardships that went with the task, and Lawson could see the future taking shape in their work — farms and plantations spreading westward from the coast, bringing hope and prosperity to an innocent land.

That was how it seemed in 1701, as the new century dawned on a world that was raw and untamed but so full of promise, particularly in comparison to the one they had left. The Gaillards shared in those feelings of hope. They were already prominent in the affairs of the colony, with Bartholomew the most visible member of the clan. He was part of a five-member committee to oversee land grants in the village of Jamestown, a new Huguenot community on the lower Santee named in honor of the English king. He was also a captain in the colonial militia, for these were uneasy times in South Carolina. They were nervous about the Spanish who lived down the coast, and nervous also about the Indian tribes all around.

The Indians were probably the most delicate problem, for they were critically important to the colonial economy. They were trading partners, swapping more than 50,000 deerskins a year for items that were made in the factories of London. The colonists were essentially the middle men in the deal, and many of them found it a profitable arrangement. The Indians, however, were growing more restless. Their lands were shrinking as the white settlers' farms spread west through the swamps, and their people were dying from strange new diseases. And too many of the European traders were cheats.

There was a story told often in the Santee basin about a tribe that grew tired of dealing with the whites. They had heard good things about the English king, who was said to be fair in his treatment of his subjects, and they decided it was time to speak with him directly. They gathered their finest deerskins and furs, and set out in an armada of dugout canoes, paddling toward the sun as it rose from the Atlantic. But the great ocean had merely swallowed them whole, leaving nothing but their grieving families behind.

By the turn of the century, many of the Indian bands had been destroyed, especially those along the coast. There was one, however, that was menacing and strong. The Yamasees under the leadership of Chief Altamaha had moved north from Florida in 1685, about the same time that the Huguenots arrived. They built a string of towns in the marshes south of Charleston, with a total population of more than 1,000. But the Yamasees were known to be unhappy — angry with the whites for encroaching on their lands, and for sending unscrupulous traders to their midst who plied the Indians with the white man's rum, then charged them exorbitant prices for more.

On April 14, 1715, with rumors of an Indian war in the air, a colonial agent named Thomas Nairne journeyed to the Yamasee village of Pocotaligo. He met with the chiefs and thought it went well, but the next morning he was seized and bound to a stake, where a Yamasee war party set him on fire. His agony echoed up and down the coast as the Yamasee attacked, killing dozens of settlers and driving hundreds more from their homes. The attacks continued well into the summer, eventually spreading north to the Santee River, where the Huguenots fled to the safety of Charleston.

There, they regrouped and helped raise an army of 1,200 men, who quickly broke the power of the Yamasee nation, driving the survivors all the way to Florida. It is almost certain that Bartholomew Gaillard played a part in the fight. As a captain in the militia he hardly could have missed it, and there were stories handed down in the family through the years of skirmishes fought in the Low Country swamplands — of musket fire and cries of pain and bodies floating facedown in the creeks. Whatever the reality, this much is certain: Bartholomew died in 1718, not long after the

Yamasee defeat. He was barely in his 50s, and he left behind a wife, Elizabeth, and five young children, the smallest of whom was a newborn baby.

But Bartholomew had managed to care for them well. He set aside a tract of land for each child, and left the main plantation to his wife. He must have taken some satisfaction in that. The family faced a future much different from its past — certainly from Bartholomew's own boyhood, which was spent in the shadow of oppression in France. Now, despite the harsh realities of America, there seemed to be nothing that they couldn't overcome.

Certainly, Theodore felt that way. He was Bartholomew's second oldest son, and easily the most ambitious of the bunch. By the time he was 30, he had added substantially to his own inheritance — buying out the share of his sister, Eleanor, and inheriting the lands of his older brother, Frederick, who died without leaving any children of his own. Theodore's main tract was in the Wambaw Swamp, six miles south of the Santee River — an area well-suited to the cultivation of rice. It had been a difficult crop for the first wave of settlers. They struggled to clear the swamps and dam the marshes, and it took them even longer to discover how to produce a high quality grain. The breakthrough came around the turn of the century with the importation of large numbers of slaves.

Many of them came from western Africa, where rice had long been a staple of the diet. Unlike their masters, they knew how to grow it. But the planters soon learned, and by the 1730s when Theodore Gaillard was getting his start, South Carolina was producing more than 20 million pounds every year. Nor was that all. By the 1740s, indigo had emerged as a major cash crop, after the seeds were imported from the West Indies. It was a staple of the British textile industry, so much in demand that the British government paid a bounty for every pound that was shipped. It made for a boom economy in the colony, and fortunes grew quickly in South Carolina, with few any larger than Theodore Gaillard's.

But there were also problems — the fear of the Indian tribes for one thing. In September of 1751, a war party raided Theodore's plantation. They struck in the night, stealing rice from his millhouse, before moving on to butcher cattle at his neighbor's. But this was a small and desperate band, particularly in comparison to the Cherokees in the west, and even they were subdued after 1760 when the colonists launched a preemptive strike, an expedition swift and cruel, burning 15 Cherokee towns. After that, the Indians were not a major worry. What concerned Theodore was the curious attitude of the colonists themselves — a growing impatience with the British empire. His neighbors, it seemed, were getting a little cocky, protesting every tax and duty from the parliament. On the specific issues he might sympathize, but something much bigger was going on here — a growing obsession with the idea of liberty, and more and more talk about open rebellion. In Theodore's mind, the idea was foolish. The British, after all, had enabled his Huguenot family to survive — and even more to the point, they paid him a handsome bounty for his indigo. There were specific issues that cried out for debate; the tax on tea, for example, had become a symbol of discontent. But in December of 1773, a group of rebels in Boston — dressed as savages, which many of the loyalists regarded as appropriate — boarded a British ship in the harbor and pitched 300 tea chests into the river. Eleven months later, there was a copycat assault in the harbor of Georgetown, S.C., and now people's passions were inflamed all around.

Early in 1775, the Provincial Congress met in Charleston, the first of three sessions in that pivotal year. Theodore's two older sons, John and Theodore Jr., were among the delegates, and so was his younger brother, Tacitus. They found themselves caught in a verbal battlefield between those who favored immediate secession and a larger group who hoped to avoid it. In the summer meeting of the congress, the debate grew bitter. Word had reached the colony in April that the British Parliament had taken a vote, vowing to suppress the rebellion by force. In that same month, the first blood was shed in Massachusetts, with small-scale skirmishes at Lexington and Concord, and the issue after that was no longer taxes, or any other fiscal policy of the parliament. The debate now turned to the notion of liberty, which was a powerful idea in the American colonies. Partly, of course, it was a British import, the gift of John Locke to the founding fathers of America, but it had other roots much closer to home.

In the South especially, the institution of slavery painted a vivid and ironic picture of tyranny, and neither the lesson nor the irony was lost. In Virginia, for example, the firebrand patriot, Patrick Henry, agonized over his own inconsistencies — his support of freedom for the American colonies, while he, himself, was the owner of slaves. "Would any one believe it?" he wrote in despair. "I will not, I cannot justify it."

In South Carolina, Henry Laurens agreed. Laurens was a man of dignity and caution, one of the most respected leaders in the South, who would soon become President of the Continental Congress. In the rush toward freedom, he wrote an anguished letter to his son, declaring his intention to emancipate his slaves, for the irony was simply too vivid to bear. In the end, of course, it was all just talk. Slavery was much too deeply entrenched, and the South was not about to let it go. But in a curious way it added an edge to the rhetoric of freedom. In the South they could see what the alternative looked like.

And yet if liberty was the battle cry of the times and the passion of the Provincial Congress in Charleston, there were delegates who felt a very different pull. All their lives they had been loyal to the king, and even on the other side of the Atlantic their duty was clear. They were English subjects first of all, and whatever their aggravations with the parliament, they wanted no part of a treasonous war.

It was a clash of imperatives — liberty on the one hand, loyalty on the other, tearing at the conscience of every man in the hall. But eventually, of course, every man had to choose, and the Gaillards drifted to the side of the king.

By the summer of 1775, they were in a minority, and it was increasingly clear that it was a dangerous place to be. On June 1, the congress issued a call to arms, pledging to "sacrifice our lives and fortunes" in the pursuit of freedom with a corollary promise to jail anybody who didn't agree. The Gaillard delegates — Tacitus, John and Theodore Jr. — worried about the growing mood of intolerance and so did their Huguenot neighbor, Henry Laurens. Perhaps it was simply a matter of background, the memory of ancestors driven from their homes, but Laurens declared in a speech to the congress that it was dangerous and wrong to judge another man's conscience.

Soon, however, his position was overwhelmed

by the fury of the times, and when the Declaration of Independence finally came, the South quickly lapsed into civil war, neighbor against neighbor, with astonishing acts of cruelty all around. For nearly five years, there was no pattern to it. John Palmer, for example, was a neighbor and close friend of the Gaillard family who was seized and tortured by a band of Tories — not for any act of his own commission, but because his young son, Thomas, had gone off to fight under Francis Marion. Palmer was old and frail, unable to resist when his tormentors dragged him off to a church and locked him in a family burial vault. He shared that gloomy prison with his brother, the two of them huddled against the cold — grateful even in the midst of their terror that the burial vault was not airtight. Eventually, they were turned loose in the swamps, and it took them nearly two days to get home, each brother occasionally carrying the other on his back whenever it seemed that they couldn't go on.

Their story was one that quickly made the rounds, but it was no worse, certainly, than ugly episodes from the other side — the story, for example, of a renegade captain under Francis Marion who decided to horsewhip a British sympathizer. Marion himself was horrified at the account — how the captain, Maurice Murphy, tied the aging Tory to a gate and demanded to know who he supported in the war.

"King George," the old man replied.

13

Murphy ordered 50 lashes with a bullwhip.

"Now who are you for?" he demanded.

When the old man refused to renounce the king, Murphy ordered 50 more lashes, then asked again and ordered 50 more. The Tory by now was close to death but still he refused to alter his allegiance. Murphy merely shrugged and left him bleeding on the ground.

That's the way it was in South Carolina — not a clean and heroic war but a bloody and unpredictable strife, where the mission of many was simply to survive. In the collective memory of the Gaillard clan, it bore a terrible resemblance to the holy wars of France, and the question they faced was what to do about it. Theodore Gaillard, who was now in his 60s, became a fierce and belligerent Tory, and his sons, John and Theodore Jr., joined him resolutely in that position. His youngest son, Peter, was a little less sure, but in the beginning he took the side of his family.

Tacitus, meanwhile, decided to leave. Sometime around 1778, he packed up his family and headed west. Traveling with a minister named Paul Turquand, he made a loop to the north around Cherokee country, where the Indians were restless trying to grasp the implications of the white man's war. After weeks of travel, they made it through the mountains of Virginia and Pennsylvania, then down the Ohio River to the Mississippi. Tragedy struck in western Tennessee. Two of the Gaillard children died and were buried in an anonymous grave before the party moved on.

Eventually, they came to New Orleans — Spanish territory, where they hoped to find freedom from the colonial civil war. Instead, they found persecution for their faith. Louisiana was Catholic, and no more tolerant of protestant heresy than the French had been under Louis XIV. Forbidden even to hold a service in his home, Tacitus rebelled and was promptly put away in a Spanish prison.

According to one account, that is where he died. According to another, he eventually made his way upriver to Natchez. Whatever the case, his ordeal in New Orleans served as a reminder, if one were needed, that his family's survival was not yet assured. For the moment at least, it must have seemed clear that not much had changed in the first 100 years.

Chapter 2
The Revolution

The agony was different for Peter Gaillard, Theodore's youngest son and the nephew of Tacitus. Born in 1757, he was not yet 20 when the revolution began, and his life before then had not been hard. He was born on his father's Wambaw Plantation, in the swamps where Joachim had established the family and where Theodore had made his fortune in rice.

Peter was 10 before he started to school and was shocked to discover how little he knew. He studied hard, partly out of shame, he later admitted, for there were boys much younger whose knowledge of the basics was much greater than his. But he caught up quickly, and after graduation he and his best friend, Samuel DuBose, went to work in Charleston. They each took jobs with Peter's older brother, Theodore Jr., a successful merchant and a leader in the colony, who was soon to be elected to the Provincial Congress.

Peter and Samuel didn't care much for Charleston. With the outbreak of war, they returned to the swamps where they began planting indigo with plans to work the plantation together. Soon, however, the revolution intervened. Samuel was stirred by the patriot cause, and with a spirited young neighbor named Thomas Palmer, he went away to fight under Francis Marion. Peter must have been tempted to join them, for Marion was a gallant figure even then — a veteran of the Cherokee wars, regarded by his men as fearless and bold. He also was connected to the Gaillard family. His brother, Job, was married to Peter's sister, Elizabeth, and Francis had been the best man in the wedding. But Peter had other things to think about. His older brothers, by now, were supporters of the British, and so was his aging father, who did not look kindly on rebellion by his sons.

At first, Peter simply tried to lay low. For a while, it worked as the war moved north, for the British failed in their first assault on the South. In June of 1776, they launched a preemptive attack on Charleston, with an armada from the most powerful navy in the world gathering just outside the harbor. But the Americans were ready. They had built a fort on Sullivans Island, a narrow spit of sand jutting out from the harbor, and though the architecture was strange, the fort was built with the British in mind. The walls were made from palmetto logs — two parallel rows with 16 feet of sand in between, designed to withstand the cannon fire of the fleet.

The battle began on June 28, and for more than nine hours the palmetto walls held. The ships, meanwhile, took a terrible pounding. Three frigates ran aground in the first minutes of the fight, getting caught in the shoals at the western edge of the harbor, and the death toll mounted as the day wore on. Finally, on the morning of June 29, the British gave up. They sailed with the tide for the open Atlantic, and it was nearly three years before they returned. But eventually, of course, they did come back, and despite his reluctance to pick a side in the war, young Peter Gaillard could no longer escape.

He knew that his moment of decision was near when new fighting started in the city of Savannah. In December of 1778, the British took control of the town, and a year after that they began their move up the coast to Charleston. By the middle of February, they had 5,000 troops just south of the city, and the reinforcements poured in for the next two months — the army swelling to more than 10,000 men. The Americans were determined to defend the city, and they, too, called for reinforcements. The problem was, there simply weren't enough. At its peak, Charleston had 6,000 defenders, and by the middle of April they were surrounded, with no hope of winning and no way to retreat from a much larger force. Their surrender came on May 12, after an artillery battle that lasted all night. "A glorious sight...a dreadful night," wrote the American general, William Moultrie, who wept at the formal surrender ceremony. He had good reason. Nearly 300 Americans were killed or wounded at the second battle of Charleston, and a staggering 5,500 were captured by the British. One of the few to escape was Francis Marion, who had broken his ankle just before the siege, and, unable to fight, had been carried off to hide in the swamps.

The British were now at a moment of truth. They still had to deal with Marion and some other scattered remnants of the American army. But with their victory at Charleston, and with another that followed that summer in Camden, they were suddenly face to face with their own most basic assumption about the war. It had long been an article of faith in the parliament that the South would eventually prove loyal to the king — especially once the might of the British army was clear. The time had come to test that assumption, and the British commander in the South, Gen. Charles Cornwallis, issued a call for every supporter of the king to step forward. Several of the Gaillards already had. Theodore Jr., the merchant, was helping to supply the British troops, and along with his older brother, John, soon accepted a commission in the loyalist militia. It was time for Peter to make up his mind, and at the urging and intercession of his father, he, too, volunteered on the side of the British. He became a captain in a small troop of cavalry — a dashing young soldier in the description of his peers, erect and strong, with high cheekbones and wind-tousled hair.

His first taste of fighting came in September of 1780. Because of his knowledge of the Santee swamps, he was second in command of a loyalist patrol assigned to hunt down Francis Marion. Marion was driving the British crazy. He and his ragtag band of men, which even included a handful of slaves fighting side by side with the others, would appear out of nowhere, disrupting supplies and attacking British outposts, generally making it harder for the army to function. When the attacks were over, they would disappear in the swamps — the tangled terrain along the Santee River where the pine forests suddenly gave way to the marsh. In the summer it was hot and infested with snakes, and in the winter it was shrouded with a cold gray mist. In any season, the British troops didn't like it. But to Peter Gaillard and the others it was home. They felt good about their chances of tracking down Marion — the Swamp Fox, as he was then known —and their hope when they started was to take him by surprise.

21

Marion, however, got word of their coming. On the starlit night of September 28, the loyalists were camped just west of a black-water creek, known to the natives as Black Mingo. There were 46 men, including Peter Gaillard and his commander, John Ball — about the same number as in Marion's patrol. Both sides understood the importance of surprise, and as midnight approached, Marion and his men were riding in silence on the narrow sand road, the moonlight casting shadows through the pines. About a mile from the camp, they came to a bridge. It was old and creaky and the planks on the floor began to rattle as Marion and his horsemen started across. The echo drifted to the loyalist camp, where Peter and his troops were startled from their sleep. The shooting began a few minutes later as Marion and his men came charging from the dark. They attacked from two sides, and after a volley or two, the loyalists panicked. According to one eyewitness account, Peter did his best to persuade them to fight. Instead, they dropped their muskets and ran — a terrified flight to the safety of the swamps. Young Peter was stunned. Like every good soldier, he had tried to prepare himself for war — for the blood and the screams and the certainty that people around him would die. But this was something else. It was a defeat sudden, graceless and bitter, and it came at a deeply unsettling time.

It was becoming clear in the fall of 1780 that

loyalists were not turning out in large numbers — and bad things were happening to those who did. Less than two weeks after the battle of Black Mingo, a blood-curdling story began to make the rounds in South Carolina. It seems that an army of more than 1,000 Tories was defeated by a patriot force at Kings Mountain. But this was no ordinary defeat. The American rebels — frontiersmen from the mountains of North Carolina — ignored the loyalists' flags of surrender and began to shoot them down in cold blood. More than 300 fell victim to the slaughter, and when the killing was finished, a group of patriots searched out the body of Patrick Ferguson, the Tory commander. They stripped it naked and began to urinate on the corpse.

The dead eventually were gathered into piles and buried together in makeshift graves, but packs of wolves soon dug them up, sharing their feast with the neighborhood hogs. It was easily the most gruesome moment in the war, chilling to the Tories of South Carolina, but it was not their only cause for alarm. By the winter of 1781, the momentum was clearly beginning to shift. The Americans in the South had a new commander, a Rhode Island Quaker named Nathaniel Greene, who was known as a brilliant military strategist. On December 2, 1780, he had ridden into Charlotte, N.C., a muddy little town with maybe two dozen houses and a log courthouse and first met the soldiers he would lead into battle. They were pathetic. Many were hungry and poorly clothed, while others were simply running amok. They drank and fought and stole what they wanted from the surrounding countryside, but with a few harsh words and a public hanging, Greene quickly restored a sense of order. He also came to the South with a plan, a strategy for confronting the army of Cornwallis. He took his cue, in part, from Francis Marion, the Swamp Fox guerilla from South Carolina. Marion would launch his deadly attacks, catching the enemy most often by surprise, and he was also the master of the skillful retreat — picking the time and place for the fight and then moving on. Greene saw no reason why a whole army couldn't do it, particularly when his own was small and tattered, clearly not in any condition for a head-to-head fight with Gen. Cornwallis.

Greene and George Washington had gone over the plan carefully. They would force the British army to chase them, fighting only when it was advantageous to Greene, while Marion and the other bands of militia attacked the British lines of supply. The strategy was political as much as military. They hoped to demonstrate to a war-weary parliament that it was simply not possible to conquer the South. There were too few Tories and the American army was still in the field, still clearly capable of putting up a fight. It was Greene's southern strategy for ending the war. The Americans would win it by refusing to lose.

Early in 1781 as the General was beginning to implement his plan, Peter Gaillard made a stunning decision. He wrote his best friend, Samuel DuBose, an officer in Francis Marion's brigade, and said he wanted to change sides in the war. Perhaps it was his personal taste of defeat — the vivid memories of the Battle of Black Mingo, combined with the general drift of the war — or perhaps it was simply what he wanted all along. Whatever the case, the final obstacle to his split with the British disappeared in 1781 with the death of his father, Theodore Gaillard. Theodore was an overbearing man — an ardent Tory who demanded the strict obedience of his family. As one neighbor put it with respect to Peter, "...the violence and uncompromising character of the father probably influenced the son."

Now, however, the influence was gone, and Peter made it clear to Samuel DuBose that he would perform any service that Francis Marion might command — "provided it involved no mortifying or humiliating feelings."

Marion accepted Peter's offer at once. For one thing, he was always short of men. His band was small, and there was an inevitable attrition that went with the war. But there was also something in Marion's character — a touch of the Huguenot spirit of Henry Laurens, who had lectured the patriots from the beginning of the revolution about the dangers of judging another man's conscience. Marion understood that these were difficult times. Good men were caught in competing ideals. Five others, in fact, had renounced the king after the Battle of Black Mingo, pledging their allegiance to Marion's brigade.

In addition to the precedent already established, Marion had admired Peter's courage in battle and not only welcomed him into the ranks, but decided also to make him a captain. He sent DuBose to lead Peter to their camp, knowing full well that some of his men would be happy to shoot a former Tory on sight. When DuBose returned with the new recruit, Marion and his staff rode out to meet them. The general was not a handsome man. He had a large hooked nose, and his chin and his hairline each tended to recede. Nevertheless, he cut quite a figure on his big sorrel gelding — a horse he had captured at Black Mingo, and in a private little irony that he seemed to enjoy had named for the Tory commander, John Ball.

Marion greeted Peter Gaillard warmly, exchanging salutes, and according to one account handed down in the family, telling him that now was his chance to make good. Peter's first opportunity came at a place called Biggin Church not far from his own indigo plantation. It had once been an Anglican house of worship, but during the war it had been transformed into a fort and a base of supplies for the British. It was also the spot where the Gaillards' aging neighbor, John Palmer, had been roughly dragged by a group of Tories and imprisoned in a family burial vault.

On July 19 just before sunrise, the British commander in the area, John Coates, began a retreat down the river toward Charleston. He put a torch to the church, destroying the store of munitions it contained, rather than allowing it to fall to the Americans. Coates knew there were patriot forces in the area, and he was determined either to make it to Charleston or to find a better place to stand and fight.

As his men trudged south through the July sun, Peter Gaillard was sent to harass them. He rode at the head of a small band of cavalry, charging periodically from the Low Country woods, until finally Col. Coates grew tired of the annoyance. He decided the time had come to fight, and his soldiers dug in at a plantation house — a formidable position at the crest of a hill with a large open field that the Americans would have to cross. Francis Marion surveyed the scene and decided against an immediate attack. He was afraid that too many of his soldiers would die. But another general, Thomas Sumter, outranked him and ordered a charge. The Americans were cut to pieces in the field.

Marion lost 50 of his men, and as the survivors limped away in defeat it must have been a bitter moment for Peter Gaillard. He had been in two battles in the American Revolution and had been on the losing side both times. This one, of course, was less disgraceful than Black Mingo, where his men had simply dropped their muskets and run. But now the images of death were all around, the bodies lying stiff and contorted in the field, and it was hard to know which reality was worse. Still, he had been lucky enough to survive, and he could take some comfort in the next several months when the news from the rest of the war was better. It seems that the British general, Cornwallis, had grown weary of the chase of Nathaniel Greene, which had gone on now for nearly a year, punctuated by some battles that nobody won. Cornwallis decided to invade Virginia, seizing control of the coastal city of Yorktown. But suddenly in the fall of 1781, Cornwallis was trapped. George Washington had moved his main army south, and before the British could respond, had surrounded Yorktown with 20,000 men.

On October 19, Cornwallis surrendered.

It was, of course, a pivotal moment in the war, for the British government quit the fight after that. On February 27, 1782, the House of Commons asked the king to end it. But the fighting didn't stop — not in the Low Country of South Carolina, where the killing went on for nearly a year and Peter Gaillard was in the middle of it. It was mop-up work for the American forces, but there were moments of terrible irony and pain.

The worst came on a hot August morning on a river south of Charleston. Peter was riding with a small patrol led by John Laurens, who was regarded by many of the founding fathers as perhaps the most promising young man in the country. He was only 27 but his resume was brilliant. He had been an aide to George Washington and an envoy to France, negotiating the terms of French support for the Revolution. He was also known as a man of great courage, not only in battle but in confronting the moral issues of the day. Already, for example, he had spoken out against slavery, once writing in a letter to his father, Henry Laurens, that those who supported that particular institution were motivated purely by their own self-interest. "Indeed," he concluded, "when driven from everything else, they generally exclaimed: Without slaves how is it possible for us to be rich?"

But if Laurens was brilliant and passionate and brave, he also was known as something of a hothead. He once had challenged an American general to a duel when he thought the general had insulted George Washington, and now in the summer of 1782 he was eager to continue the fight with the British. He knew, of course, that the war was won, but as long as there were troops on American soil, Laurens was determined to drive them to the sea. He got word on the night of August 26 of a British patrol heading south from Charleston. The British were merely looking for rice to help feed the hungry garrison in the city. Laurens, however, decided to attack. He gathered a force of 50 horse soldiers and set out in the early morning hours, unaware that the British had gotten word of his coming. They were waiting in the marsh of the Combahee River, at a loop just north of the city of Beaufort, when Laurens and his men came riding into sight. It was not yet dawn. The marsh was quiet as the Americans trotted along the roadway. Laurens rode at the head of the column, with Peter Gaillard close at his side. Suddenly, they noticed the British in the grass, seeing them only when they rose to fire. There was less than a second for Laurens to decide: surrender, attack or try to escape. With those as his options, Laurens attacked. He spurred his horse, called for a charge, and was cut from the saddle in the first wave of bullets.

His death was one of the last in the war, mourned universally by the men he served. "He had not a fault," wrote his mentor, George Washington, "unless intrepidity bordering on rashness could come under that denomination...."

As for Peter Gaillard, once again he survived. He must have wondered at his own good fortune, and indeed there is evidence from the rest of his life that his luck was something he never took for granted. He easily could have died, or remained with his family on the side of the British. Instead, despite his uncertainty and doubt, he had cast his lot with the winning side — arriving at that position in time to share in the jubilation of the patriots when the last British ship had sailed out of Charleston.

In the weeks after that, he made his way home to the Santee River and married his sweetheart, Elizabeth Porcher. He put in his crops of indigo and rice, and the future at the moment must have seemed pretty bright. In these months at the end of the Revolutionary War, Peter Gaillard was a grateful survivor. It was a feeling and a way of looking at the world that would become the signature of his life.

Sketch of The Rocks by Peter Gaillard's great-great-great-great-granddaughter, Tracy Gaillard

Chapter 3
The Gift of Captain Peter

The first few years of peace were hard. It was clear despite the euphoria of freedom that the wounds ran deep in South Carolina. For awhile at least, Peter Gaillard encountered suspicion and even occasional insults from his neighbors, who regarded him as Benedict Arnold in reverse.

But his life was easier than that of his brothers who had maintained their support of the British to the end. Some of the most ardent Tories had fled, moving to England or the West Indies, while others had remained and tried to stave off ruin. John Gaillard was one of the latter. He was Peter's oldest brother, a handsome man who carried himself with an air of calm. His property had been seized under the Confiscation Act of 1782, which stripped the most prominent Tories of their land. But two years later he was allowed to appeal. On February 14, 1784, he appeared before a committee of his peers to answer the "heavy accusations" against him. The most serious of those was that he had helped arm slaves who had succeeded in burning a neighbor's house. John denied it and presented witnesses to support his position. The committee was impressed. His answers were clear and cogent and strong, and when the hearing was over most of John's property had been restored.

In the minds of many of his neighbors and family, he became a symbol of reconciliation, taking his place once again in the life of his community. Though he didn't live to see it, barely 20 years after the confiscation of his property his son was elected to the U.S. Senate, and the political restoration of the family was complete.

The economy, however, was a whole different story. Part of it was simply the retribution of the British. When the war was over, they stopped paying bounties on American indigo, which had become the margin of profit for the planters. About the same time, the weather turned treacherous, with so much flooding along the Santee River that the crops rotted year after year in the fields. Once, at Peter Gaillard's plantation the entire yield consisted of a few bushels of corn, and he was forced to support his family and slaves in a season when he earned no money at all. He borrowed to do it, though he had no income to pay off his debts, and as his neighbor Frederick Porcher later put it, "ruin appeared to stare him in the face."

Peter was not alone in that. All across the Low Country of South Carolina, many people wondered if the plantations were doomed, and some even questioned the future of slavery — not because of what it was doing to blacks, but because of the economic burden on the planters.

Peter, meanwhile, simply tried to pay his debts. He first offered pieces of his land for sale, and when he found no takers, his only option was to begin selling slaves. He had inherited 58 from his father, and another 48 from the family of his wife. The market was down — less than $300 for a good field hand — but when Peter offered to sell most of his, trying to raise what money he could, his creditors were impressed with his good faith gesture and agreed to grant him an extension on his debt.

It was about this time that he took the biggest gamble of his life. Without knowing how he was going to pay for it, he decided to buy another piece of land — a tract of higher ground on the western Santee, where the Low Country swamps gave way to the pines and his crops might survive the hard winter rains. The purchase price was $3,000, to be paid in annual installments of $1,000. As the first payment loomed, Peter had no money. In desperation, he bought a lottery ticket in Charleston, and was stunned a few days later when he won — a prize of exactly $1,000.

Peter made his payment, and he had to hope now that his new tract was fertile, and that he could find a crop well suited to the soil. He decided to try cotton. Nobody had grown it in that part of the state, but Peter knew that he had to do something. He began with a type of long-staple seed, not knowing whether it would produce in that climate, and to his amazement, once again, it worked. Peter could hardly believe his luck — not that he hadn't worked hard to create it, but who could have known that he would win the lottery, or that a cotton crop would take root and flourish in a land where no one else had ever grown it?

The line of survival could be so thin, so tenuous and inexplicable sometimes, as it had been in the war when he had seen his comrades die on every side. But survival this time was not Peter's alone. His discovery raised new hopes among the Low Country planters — new economic possibilities for his state — particularly because of the time at which it happened.

Three years earlier, a young inventor named Eli Whitney had come south in search of a teaching job. He was staying in Savannah as the guest of Catherine Greene, the widow of Nathaniel, who had commanded the Southern forces in the Revolutionary War. One night over dinner the conversation turned to the subject of cotton. Her other guests agreed that it could be the salvation of the planters in the South if only something could be done about the seeds. They were green and sticky and almost impossible to remove from the fiber. Over the clink of glasses and the murmur of conversation, Mrs. Greene smiled and offered a solution. "Mr. Whitney," she said, "can make a machine...."

By the following spring, Mr. Whitney had done it. In April of 1793, he unveiled the cotton gin, as he called it — a set of wire teeth that were mounted on a cylinder and pulled the fiber through slots too narrow for the seeds. It was clear immediately that it was a stroke of genius, though from Whitney's point of view there was a frustrating flaw. The machine was so simple and easy to build that planters all over the South began to steal it.

Peter Gaillard may have been one of those. Whether he bought it from Whitney or built it himself, he had a gin for the harvest of 1796, spitting out more cotton in half an hour than an army of his slaves could clean in a day. The cotton market took off after that and Peter rode with it. By 1800, he was out of debt, and a few years later, he was one of the wealthiest men in the state — accustomed once again to the comfort and prosperity he had known as a boy.

In 1803, he started building a house — a great columned mansion on his new piece of land. He clearly wanted it to be something special, for he was involved in the planning of every detail, keeping meticulous notes on the progress. On May 11, Peter and his slaves cut down a cypress tree near the river and began to split it into shingles — 6,500 before they were through. On September 1, they began making bricks, and on November 21, Peter hired a carpenter at $1.50 a day and soon began planning the interior of the house. He wanted the mantels to be genteel — not ostentatious, he was careful to say, but carved with a grace that was pleasing to the eye. It was a job that Peter himself might have done. He was fond of carving every night after supper, sitting on his porch with a cypress shingle, most often delivered by one of his servants, and slowly whittling it into a shape. Sometimes he was more ambitious than that, carving the balustrades at other houses where he'd lived. But not this time — not at the Rocks, as the new place was called. This time the standard was a little bit higher, and when the work was finished in 1805, Peter was pleased with the overall result. The house was handsome with its six white columns and avenue of oaks. It had two ponds behind it, and was flanked by gardens of roses on the sides.

To the casual eye, it might have seemed extravagant — "with even an appearance of wasteful profusion," as Peter's son, Thomas, later wrote in his memoirs. But Thomas saw his father's aims as aesthetic, and if beauty was Peter's translation of his wealth, it was a celebration not of his personal achievements but of the inexplicable good fortune of his life. He had survived the war and the possibility of ruin, and now he was raising splendid crops every year and buying plantations to give to his sons. Peter had eight children overall, three of them daughters, and in the early years of the 1800s, he provided land for the boys and houses in Charleston for each of the girls.

And of course he also provided them with slaves. In the South at that time, there was no more important measure of wealth, and Peter's field hands now numbered in the hundreds. He seems not to have worried about it much — not to have agonized over the institution itself, which in fact was debated quite vigorously at times. In 1795, a group of Low Country ministers — 23 in all — drew up a strongly worded resolution, condemning the "impropriety and evil of slavery...and its baneful consequences on religious society." It was an echo of the voices from the American Revolution — Patrick Henry, Henry Laurens and others — who understood the screaming inconsistency between slavery and the principles on which the revolution was based. There were slaves in every colony at the time, but the institution quickly receded to the South — and even there, after the turn of the century, there were more organized abolitionist activities than in the North.

The abolitionists, however, faced an uphill

climb. The cotton culture, buttressed by the invention of Eli Whitney and the discoveries of planters like Peter Gaillard, gave slavery new life — made it, again, a centerpiece of the economy. For many Southern planters, slaves were the most visible symbol of success, and among the richest families in the South, they represented an enormous investment of money. Even Henry Laurens was worried about it, as he began to consider the possibility of manumission. "What will my children say," he wrote to his son, "if I deprive them of so much estate?"

In one form or another, it was a question that a great many Southerners asked. But there was another driving force behind the institution of slavery, a consideration much stronger than any issue of economics. Essentially, it had to do with fear. What would happen if the slaves were set free? It was the other great dilemma that haunted the South, even those leaders with little use for the system. John Laurens, for example, had long been an advocate of emancipation, proposing early in the Revolutionary War that slaves be armed to fight the British and then set free as a reward for their service. But even Laurens worried about the result — the Low Country suddenly teeming with blacks, roaming uncontrolled in the land of their masters. "The example of Rome," he wrote to his father, "is a warning to us to proceed with caution.... We have sunk the African and their descendants below the standard of humanity, and almost rendered them incapable of that blessing which Heaven has bestow'd upon us all."

Laurens blamed slavery for the degradation of blacks. Others around him were less reflective. In the words of historian Joel Williamson, white culture was tied to color and blood, and blackness was a symbol of inferiority — even of a savagery that had to be controlled in a people so recently removed from the jungle. Given that, emancipation was an invitation to disaster — a danger far more terrible to consider than the troubling but time-honored institution of slavery.

It was a point of view that hardened with the passage of time, and Peter Gaillard had his own answer to it. He did his best to make slavery benign. That, at least, was an article of faith in the family, carefully preserved and handed down through the years. A genealogy written by his great-grandson praises Peter's "warm feelings" toward his slaves and ends on a note of sweeping reassurance: "His servants...knew no Simon Legree."

Actually, that may be close to the truth. In 1982, Cheryll Ann Cody of the University of Minnesota made a detailed study of Peter's plantation records, trying to discover what she could about his slaves. Her reviews are mixed, but Peter emerges quite clearly as a man of principle, particularly in his respect for the integrity of slave families. He subjected them to no derogatory nicknames, and even at times of purchase or sale generally did his best to keep them together. His principles were essentially an extension of his father's. In his will when he died in 1781, Theodore Gaillard stipulated with regard to his slaves: "The Negroes...are not to be parted from their father or mother under the age of 14 years."

For Peter, that was part of a broader pattern in which nuclear families remained intact, husbands and wives were not separated, and small children nearly always remained with their parents. But when Peter was handing out slaves to his children, extended families sometimes were divided. Brothers and sisters and sons who were over the age of 14 often wound up at different plantations. In many cases, the plantations were less than 20 miles apart, but given the limited mobility of the slaves, the separations were wrenching — a source of pain, writes Cheryll Ann Cody, "even under the best of circumstances."

All of this Peter recorded in his notes — a plantation ledger that he kept through the years, tracing the births and deaths of his slaves, the payment of his taxes, his various experiments in the cultivation of his crops. His looping script is legible today, recording the satisfaction he felt when he discovered in 1811, for example, that cotton plants 18 inches apart did better than those growing closer together.

"It remains to be proved," Peter noted to himself, "whether 2 feet apart would not still be better, which I shall attempt by next year if I live so long."

Because of his experiments and meticulous notations regarding the results, Peter was widely regarded by his peers as one of the most skillful planters in the state. "I never knew one better," wrote Samuel DuBose, and the local historian, Frederick Porcher, said Peter's theories on cotton were "still quoted with respect" 20 years from his death.

Thomas Gaillard, Peter's middle son, saw another ingredient in his father's success — a sobriety of judgment that, as Thomas understood it, was rooted quite simply in Peter's lack of greed. He was lenient toward those who owed him money, perhaps in memory of his own hard times, but even more than that, he never seemed tempted by the lure of sudden profit. "Speculation," wrote Thomas, "was never permitted to bias his views, or to excite him to action. His expectations were never sanguine, his calculations never extravagant." It was true, of course, Peter took risks, as when he first bought the Rocks with no money in the bank and put in his original crop of cotton. But those were desperate and uncertain experiments, motivated essentially by the need to survive. After that time, Peter worked hard at his occupation, enjoying the comforts that came his way and believing that a man didn't need any more.

He became morose when he had to give it up, when infirmities overtook him at the age of 69 and he retreated full-time to his house in Charleston. He ventured out occasionally to visit his daughters, making the short walk up East Bay Street, past the carriage paths and low-hanging oaks, with the salt breeze drifting off the harbor. He was proud of his children — the eight who had made it past the first months of life — but he thought sometimes about the four who didn't, and his three pretty wives who were also gone. First Elizabeth, then Annie and Mary. He had outlived them all, and now in the beginning of his seventh decade, he could feel his own health beginning to fail. But Peter wasn't bitter. It had been a good life all in all, full of beauty and success, even a touch of adventure in the war when he had ridden the Low Country with his neighbor, Francis Marion. And whatever the rewards that had come his way, he simply couldn't bring himself to take the credit. These things were a gift, as inexplicable to Peter as his own survival, or his recovery from ruin in the early years of independence.

One night in November of 1830, he sat down to write a short letter to his heirs, seeking, he said, to draw the curtain on his life: "I am well aware that I shall not live much longer; and have therefore thought fit to leave this paper containing some directions for the performance of the last friendly offices toward me...."

"Immediately after my decease, let my body be laid in a tight, plain coffin and sent off to St. Stephen's Church, there be interred with my wife and children, and as near the former as can conveniently be done — the funeral service being first performed at my house in Charleston, attended by some of my relatives with the least possible parade....

"It is not my wish that my death should be published in any newspaper. My friends will know it soon enough and it is of no consequence to the community.

"I cannot but here offer up, at this moment as it were of my departure, my most unfeigned thanks and grateful acknowledgements to the Supreme Ruler of the Universe for the uncommon share of health, prosperity and happiness that I have been permitted to enjoy in the course of my long life; and humbly hope that my conduct here has been such as may entitle me to favor hereafter. I may be deceived, for the very wisest of us are but in utter darkness as respects our knowledge of futurity. But I entertain the strongest hope. I feel no remorse of conscience. I feel no apprehension...."

And then he added one last note: "This remark is intended for my family...."

The letter was passed through the next generations, and gratitude became Peter's gift to his heirs. It was a feeling that seemed to grow stronger with the years, as the generations in a line from

Peter to the present defined themselves in the memory of his example. There was a pride in the family's position and achievements, tempered by the nature of Peter's understanding, and the duty of each generation to pass it on. For some of the people in the long line that followed, the duty was more of a burden than a gift. But it was also at the heart of their sense of character, and it became the source of the family's liberation, an escape from the perennial afflictions of the rich: the ingratitude and vanity and disillusionments born out of wanting even more.

Such was the legacy of Peter Gaillard, who, above all else that he accomplished in his life, came to understand the meaning of his luck.

Chapter 4
The Politics of Slavery

The legacy was tested in the next generation, particularly in the case of Peter's middle son, Thomas, who struggled all his life with feelings of failure. In a way, that was strange, for Thomas was brilliant — a writer, scholar, politician and planter who began his education in a log schoolhouse. It was a rough-hewn building just east of the church in the little town of Pineville, S.C. The teacher was a stern and hard-bitten woman, "the terror of all the wayward urchins," as Thomas later put it, dispensing the rudiments of a frontier education with all the energy and firmness she could muster. But the lessons stuck, and at the age of 13, Thomas moved away from the log schoolhouse. He spent the next two years at a prep school in New Jersey, then returned to the College of South Carolina, where he became a freshman at the age of 15, and three years later, was the valedictorian.

From the beginning, he knew that he wanted to write, and his first publication came in 1812. Imitating the style of a Roman orator — a deliberate affectation, he admitted — he drafted a letter of endorsement for his first cousin, John, who was seeking reelection to the U.S. Senate. Thomas at the time was 22, and he remembered being pleased with the public response. He enjoyed the give and take of debate, and some people said that he ought to be a lawyer. But Thomas didn't care for that particular profession, even though he seemed to have the attributes for it. He was a gifted speaker, fluent and clear, a handsome young man with sandy brown hair and sensitive eyes and the trace of a paradox in his character. He was both confident and modest in front of a crowd, easy on his feet, though basically shy, and not especially drawn to the "litigious disputations" of the law.

He settled instead on the life of a planter — a quieter calling, he thought when he started, and one that his father had mastered with grace. Thomas, however, was not very good at it. In 1813, he barely made a crop. His cotton plants withered in the hot August sun, and a September windstorm battered what was left. The following season was not a lot better, but the weather improved in 1816 and the European market for cotton was strong.

Thomas was momentarily a wealthy man, and as the money poured in, he decided to spend it — seized, he said, by the "spirit of speculation." In 1817, he bought 50 slaves at a staggering cost of $25,000. He had to borrow the money to do it, and almost immediately his luck turned sour. Twenty of his Negroes promptly died, and after three straight years of difficult weather, the cotton market crashed in 1820.

Thomas, by now, was deeply in debt and despondent at his lack of judgment and restraint. It was a humbling departure from the habits of his father, who had had his own bouts with bad weather and markets and somehow managed to ride out the storm. Embarrassed by the contrast, Thomas blamed nobody but himself. "I aggravated my misfortune," he wrote, "by injudicious management, impracticable schemes and visionary speculations. I was one who acted unwisely."

Other parts of his life were difficult as well. In 1812, he had married his neighbor, Marianne Palmer, a dark-haired woman, strong-willed and pretty, who had her share of Low Country suitors. Together, they began to raise a family, but two of their first three children died, and two more followed in the next decade. Thomas tried to bear his afflictions with grace, resigning himself as best he could to the hard and inscrutable purposes of God. He also found another calling for his life. He ran for the legislature in 1816, was elected and served until 1820, and was elected again in 1826. He was aware of the flaws and mendacity of the system, but nevertheless saw it as a noble arena — the place where the great moral issues were debated and the destiny of a nation was molded in the process.

In South Carolina, the issues were intense, particularly in 1828 when a complex crisis began to take shape. Ostensibly, the issue was a new protective tariff, designed to shield the manufacturers of New England from their more established competitors overseas. The tariff was unpopular in South Carolina, where the planters and cotton exporters of Charleston were afraid it would trigger a trade war with England. But easily the most volatile issue in the mix was one that many Southerners did not want to talk about. More and more, they were worried about an assault on slavery, especially if a strong national government in Washington began to exert its power against the South. That seemed to be happening in the case of the tariff, which was more an inconvenience than a life-and-death threat. But what if the hated abolitionists of New England — more outspoken than they had ever been before — began to sway the president and the members of congress?

The idea sent a shiver through the leaders of the South, where the prevailing attitudes about slavery were changing. They were harder now than they had been in the past, and part of it was simply a matter of fear. All across the South there were rumors of insurrection, and the terror was strong in South Carolina, where a black carpenter in Charleston, Denmark Vesey, began plotting a revolt in 1823. According to the testimony of other slaves, Vesey planned to seize control of the city then sail to Haiti with his liberated army. But his plot was discovered, and Vesey was hung. Some whites breathed a little easier after that, but suddenly in the summer of 1831 the nightmare was real. On August 21, a Sunday night in Southampton, Virginia, a band of slaves with Nat Turner at the head armed themselves with axes and knives and a few crude guns and set out on a desperate mission of slaughter. For nearly 24 hours, they hacked to death every white person they could find — nearly five dozen men, women and children, some of them slave owners, some of them not. Turner and Vesey had one thing in common. Both of them could read — and after the Turner uprising was quelled, with most of the perpetrators captured and hung, many whites were convinced that abolitionists were to blame.

Certainly, it was true that abolitionist writings were being shipped to the South from New England and other places, and the tone was different than it had been in the past. Slavery was no longer seen as a dilemma, a complex issue to be settled over time, but rather as the ultimate expression of evil.

Easily the most passionate proponent of that view was William Lloyd Garrison, a humorless crusader who hated whiskey, war and the oppression of women, but nothing so much as the institution of slavery. Garrison was not a man who made a lot of friends. He was a Massachusetts radical who survived the broken home of his boyhood and lashed out against evil everywhere he could find it. In Garrison's demonology, there were no more despicable perpetrators of wrong than the white men of the South, who enslaved other people in their own pursuit of wealth. Garrison favored immediate abolition with no compensation for the Southern planters, who had no right to own slaves in the first place.

To many leaders in the South, including Thomas Gaillard, it was a vile and inexplicable assault — even harder to understand than the aimless butchery of Nat Turner. Southerners may have agonized in the past, wondering at least in the privacy of their hearts about the contradictions inherent in the institution of slavery. But now they were caught in a whole new emotion, a defensiveness that would only grow deeper with the years and give shape to the South as a region set apart. Part of it may have been rooted in guilt, a secret knowledge of the flaw at the heart of Southern life. But the abolitionists created a backlash of denial, and in their shrillness, gave a glimmer of credibility to the Southern defense. "God knows," wrote

Thomas Gaillard's wife, Marianne, "we are not the devils they make us out to be."

All of that inflamed the constitutional crisis that began in 1828 and escalated over the next four years to push the country to the brink of civil war. In response to the tariff that was passed in that year, a document called the "South Carolina Exposition and Protest" began to circulate across the state, asserting that South Carolina, as a sovereign entity, had the right to "nullify" the tariff—simply to declare that it didn't apply. At first, nobody claimed responsibility for the document, but it was widely whispered among the Low Country planters that the author was none other than John C. Calhoun, South Carolina's most successful politician, who was then the Vice President of the United States. Certainly, the theory had Calhoun's stamp. It was a brilliant and tightly reasoned argument, and Calhoun was a political genius of sorts, ambitious and vain and ferocious in his style, with small, piercing eyes and a wild shock of hair. Later, he admitted his authorship, arguing essentially that since the states had created the national government, they had a right to overrule it whenever they chose.

To Thomas Gaillard, the theory was appalling. Like Calhoun, he was worried about the power of the federal government, especially as it began to tilt against the South. But nullification made the government a sham, reducing its laws to mere suggestions and inviting a kind of anarchy among the states. In the summer of 1828, Thomas began writing his own opinions on the subject, published first in the *Charleston Courier* and later reprinted in the *National Intelligencer*. He agreed with Calhoun that individual states had created the union, and thus every state had a right to secede. But the union also was a sacred pact, and unless a state felt driven to leave it, all citizens were bound by the national laws. Otherwise, there could be no union at all.

Thomas understood that he was playing with fire, for his arcane and rational theories of government were tied inevitably to the passions of the day, and by 1830 those passions were intense. They had grown stronger with the approach of the legislative elections, in which Thomas once again was a candidate. He had been elected in the past every time he had run, for there was something about him that the voters found appealing. He was a gentleman politician, articulate and calm, regarded by his neighbors as moderate and fair. That was his image again this time, but in 1830 it was no longer in fashion. Thomas was a candidate of the Unionist party, which opposed the theories of nullification and the tide of anger that was sweeping through the state. He understood the risk and was willing to take it but was nevertheless startled by his margin of defeat. After years of success, he was beaten two to one, and the debate leading up to the election was ugly. Many of the Unionists were branded as cowards — "submissionists" in the words of one angry editor — too timid to take a stand for the honor of the South.

It was a painful moment for Thomas Gaillard. Then as later, he was certain in his heart that his opponents were wrong, risking civil war in their assault on the union, and his integrity was more important to him than success. But it was also true that he had failed to make his case, his position overwhelmed by the passion of the times, and his defeat was compounded by other problems in his life — the lingering debts from his failures as a planter. As the drama continued in South Carolina, federal troops massing in the forts around Charleston, threatening force if necessary in support of the tariff, Thomas began making his plans to move.

The year after his defeat, he journeyed overland to the Southern frontier and found land on the bluffs of the Alabama River. It was a beautiful spot near the town of Claiborne, on a broad and graceful curve in the river with 100-foot cliffs to the water below. Thomas bought a tract of 8,000 acres, covered at the time in hardwood and pine, then returned to South Carolina for his family. It was a terrible uprooting for his wife, Marianne, who grieved off and on for the rest of her life. But Thomas was determined to make a new start — to put his financial embarrassments behind him and stay clear of politics once and for all. He had heard good things about the state of Alabama. The land was fertile and the climate less oppressive than the one they were leaving in South Carolina. But more than anything else it was new. To Thomas Gaillard in 1831, nothing was more important than that. There were times when a man simply needed a change.

Part II
New Frontiers

Thomas and Marianne Gaillard

Chapter 5
Alabama

They made the journey in the winter of 1832. The trip itself went smoothly enough, the family strung out in a small wagon train along the muddy roads of Georgia and central Alabama. Thomas Gaillard felt relief at the closing of a chapter, but it was also clear that other troubles lay ahead. These were jittery times in Alabama. There were rumors, once again, of an Indian uprising, and many of their neighbors well remembered the last one.

It began in earnest in 1813, when a band of Creeks stormed the gates of Fort Mims, a flimsy stockade just north of Mobile. The Creeks were led by William Weatherford, the son of a Scottish trader and an Indian princess. His Indian name was

Red Eagle, and he was one of those present in 1811 when the great chief Tecumseh of the Shawnee Nation came south to build a confederacy against the whites. Tecumseh visited the Cherokees and the Creeks, calling for a massive war of resistance if that was what it took to save the red man's land. Weatherford thought Tecumseh was a fool. He knew from the testimony of his father that there were too many whites for the Indians to fight. But when the die was cast, he defined himself as a Creek.

The fatal moment came on July 27, 1813. A patrol of Mississippi militia, fearing that a war with the Indians was imminent, attacked a party of Creeks on the road to Pensacola. In revenge, the Creeks attacked Fort Mims, storming through the gates at noon and killing every man, woman and child they could find. According to many historical accounts, Weatherford himself was appalled at the carnage. On the night before the battle, he had counseled against the massacre of women and children, and he knew when it happened that it would only add fury to the white man's revenge. Weatherford was right. In Tennessee, the legislature commissioned Gen. Andrew Jackson to go forth and "exterminate the Creek nation."

Jackson was joined in that undertaking by forces from Mississippi and Georgia, and in less than a year the Creeks were defeated. The last battle came at Horseshoe Bend, beginning in a meadow on the Tallapoosa River, where more than 800 Indians were killed. "The carnage was dreadful," Jackson wrote to his wife, but he said he was certain that the Creek war was over.

For 20 years, it was. William Weatherford surrendered soon after the battle and retired to his farm in southern Alabama, not far from the land that Thomas Gaillard bought. He lived there quietly until his death and urged other Creeks to do the same. But the whites kept coming, kept demanding Creek land, and by the 1830s, Gen. Jackson was president. He ordered the removal of the Creeks from Alabama, and in the days just before their Trail of Tears, they rebelled in the eastern part of the state. They burned a few houses and the toll bridge to Georgia, but the fighting ended quickly and never spread west to the town of Claiborne.

It was a reminder, however, if one were needed, that this was a rough new land that the Gaillards had entered. Thomas, in fact, was astounded by its character. In 1837, he wrote a letter to his brother, noting that even the gentry in Alabama went armed. There had been three murders in the town of Claiborne, and Thomas was alone among his neighbors in attending public meetings "without some instrument of an offensive nature." He said he was considering a move to Texas, though he wondered if things were any better there. "I feel," he wrote, with a touch of despair, "that I shall not, on this side of the grave, have a local home — a little spot of ground more endeared to me than any other."

Marianne, too, was feeling the pain. Like many other women on the Southern frontier, she longed for the old familiar landscape — the people and sights and sounds of her home. "I feel sometimes," she wrote to her brother, "that I am an inhabitant of another world, a solitary, lonely being...." She was also worried about her children. Four had died in South Carolina, but she had brought seven with her to Alabama, and two more were born soon after they arrived. For the most part, all nine of the survivors were healthy, but then in the summer of 1844, her youngest son Peter came down with a tapeworm. He went to bed one night, and the following morning he didn't wake up. His mother called to him and got no reply. He lapsed into spasms as she rushed to his bed. Marianne couldn't believe it at first — another of her children about to be lost. Peter was only seven years old, a frail little boy in comparison to the others, and the doctor at one point thought he was gone. But Peter passed the worm, a hideous creature in Marianne's description, flat and pale and several yards in length. Slowly, the child began to recover, and Marianne was able to breathe after that. "I feel so grateful," she wrote to her brother, "that I think I can endure any trouble now."

But the troubles kept coming, and after a while

the greatest burden of all was familiar, a repetition of their struggles in South Carolina. Her husband was failing once again as a planter. It hadn't been that way at first. Thomas made good crops for the first several years — so bountiful, in fact, that even the Panic of 1837 was nothing much more than an inconvenience. But the caterpillars came in 1843 — great hordes suddenly appearing in the fields, a sickening apparition as they swarmed from one cotton row to another, gorging themselves until every stalk was bare.

Thomas was forced to borrow money to survive, and he found it difficult to pay off his debt. He first offered pieces of his land for sale, and finding few takers, he began to sell his slaves. Marianne wept as they were taken away. "I thought it a great affliction...." she wrote. "I cannot part with them as though they were cattle." But she was far more worried about her husband, who seemed so strong and stoic at first, bearing his reverses with Christian resignation, while she was a bundle of nerves. But then it began to frighten her a little. Thomas grew quieter and more resigned, until suddenly she feared that he had given up entirely.

In her misery, she retreated into piety and grief, writing letter after letter to South Carolina, troubled by the painful limits of her faith. "My race is nearly done," she wrote. "I must try to get the better of my fears and trust more to Providence....But my nature is frail, and the wicked thought rises, has God brought us here to bring us down — to strip us of our earthly possessions?"

It is clear from his letters that Thomas, also, was feeling the strain, but he had been there before. It was part of the ebb and flow of life, and he did his best to find other solace. In South Carolina, he had found it in the rigors of political debate, and he still cared deeply about the affairs of the country — fearing, along with many of his neighbors, the drift of national opinion against the South.

Now, however, he kept his political opinions to himself, having lost any appetite for debate. Instead, he turned his attentions to the past. In 1845, he decided to write a history of the Huguenots of South Carolina, but the project grew in the course of his studies until it became a three-volume history of the church. The first installment was published in 1846 — 338 pages written in a period of just under six months. Thomas was afraid it was a little too broad, covering 15 centuries of ancient Christianity, but the second volume seemed to be just right. It was tightly focused, describing the Protestant Reformation of the 16th century in a style that was strong and graceful and clear.

When the book appeared in 1847, Thomas took his place among the American men of letters, and for awhile was proud of what he had done. Slowly, however, his writing became another source of frustration. By the end of the decade of the 1840s,

the third volume of his trilogy was almost done —
256 pages in an elegant script that bore a striking
resemblance to his father's. He traced the Protestants from Europe to the United States, through the
time when they got off the boat in Charleston. But
as he labored day after day at his desk — a stiff
wooden chair with one arm wide enough for his
papers — he grew increasingly unhappy with what
he had written. He brooded about it in the stillness
of his library, surrounded by the musty smell of his
books, then brooded some more as he wandered
the grounds of his river plantation, beneath the
dappled canopy of the chinaberry trees. Finally,
one day he could no longer stand it. In a fit of
gloom, he carried his manuscript to the fire, and
"consigned it page by page to the flames," watch-
ing as his labors turned slowly into ash. Once
again, he had come up short. It seemed, by now, to
be a pattern in his life — those intermingled
periods of frustration and success, when he gave it
his best, but never quite seemed to be the master of
his calling.

Sometimes he longed to let it all go — maybe
rush off to the Mexican War. "I'm a sorry marks-
man," he wrote, but something inside him yearned
for the fight. He resisted such exotic temptations,
however, contenting himself with letters from his
sons who had succumbed to the lure of the California gold rush. They were good strong boys, the
three who decided to go to California. Edmund

was a doctor, now well established in his Alabama practice; Richebourg, a graduate of Yale, had become a lawyer, brash with his opinions about anything political; and Sam, who would soon become a doctor, probably was the most steady and solid of the three. It was surprising, in a way, that they would chase after gold, hopping a freighter for the trip to Panama, then hacking their way through the mountainous jungles, and up the Pacific coast to San Francisco. They didn't find much treasure, but they returned full of tales of the California mountains — the big game hunts and cold, rocky streams and the tedious search for golden powder in the sand. It was the kind of adventure a young man should have, but when they came home to the South of the 1850s, their father had reason to worry about the future.

Thomas knew that the drift of the country was bad, for it was still caught up in the politics of slavery, and he was as guilty as anyone. It was hard to imagine the South without slaves. What would happen to the economy and the culture? But the tide of opinion was building in the North, and the condemnations were becoming more shrill.

With the election of Lincoln in 1860 — a gift of the Democrats, who couldn't agree on a candidate — the rhetoric of secession grew louder in the South, and Thomas, once again, was frightened by the sound. In South Carolina, he had staked his political career on the Union, and now as the father

66

of six grown sons, he had reason to fear a bloody civil war. But he also had other things on his mind, for the tragedies, now, were coming at him in a rush. Late in the winter of 1860, his oldest son, John, had suddenly died. He was only 46, a vigorous man, who had gone duck-hunting on a cold winter day and stayed too long in the icy water. When he returned, an inexplicable paralysis began to spread through his body and grew steadily worse until it simply consumed him.

Six months later, Thomas lost Marianne. She was stricken on the shores of Mobile Bay, where they had gone to spend the summer of 1860. At 7 in the evening of July 26, she was fishing with a group of her friends on the wharf, a favorite pastime, when she was gripped by a terrible pain in her chest. Twenty minutes later she was dead. Thomas had trouble believing it at first. He knew she had long had a troublesome heart — palpitations that seized her in moments of distress — but she had seemed much happier in the past few years, especially in the time they had spent in Mobile. It was a beautiful city of 20,000 people, with live oak canopies on the downtown streets, and the great social galas that Marianne loved — the balls and dinners and black-tie evenings, where she could shine as she had in South Carolina. Thomas was glad to see her happy; she had spent so many of her days in pain. But now she was gone, and Thomas was alone — his isolation made worse because he was deaf, living his days in a world of silence where even his grandchildren's laughter was lost.

Secession came a few months later, with South Carolina the first to go. Alabama was fourth, behind Mississippi and Florida, and as the new Confederacy began to take shape, Thomas felt a certain pride in the cause. He had never wanted it to come to this, but now that the moment of crisis was at hand, the struggle ahead seemed noble and good — an echo, really, of the American Revolution when the country stood tall in the defense of its freedom. That was the feeling they had in the South, a hatred of tyranny from a faraway place, and on the day that Alabama seceded, January 12, 1861, Thomas put a row of candles in his window.

It was his own small gesture in support of the war, for it was clear that Abraham Lincoln would fight. Thomas was uneasy about the odds; the North had the factories and population to win, if Lincoln and his generals could muster the will. That was the primary hope of the South — the fundamental strategy of the Confederacy's new president, Jefferson Davis. He would try to hold out for as long as he could, relying on the bravery of the young men of the South, and hope that the Yankees would grow weary of the fight. It was, after all, the South, not the North, that was being invaded, and perhaps the people of New York and other places would simply get enough of the whole adventure.

While the theory was being tested, Thomas could only wait and worry about his sons, who were soon dispersed to every corner of the war. Franklin, the second youngest, was fighting in Virginia under Gen. Beauregard. He was an impressive young man with hollow-looking cheeks and wind-blown hair, who had gone back to South Carolina for school and hadn't seen his father since 1853. But their letters were frequent, even during the war, and on August 4, 1861, Franklin wrote home about his first taste of fighting. The Battle of Bull Run was a bloody affair — 5,000 soldiers either wounded or killed by weapons more terrible than the world had ever seen: rifles that were accurate at 300 yards, cutting down charging soldiers like wheat.

Franklin and his men were retreating slowly on that hot summer morning in northern Virginia, until reinforcements came, and then they attacked. One of their generals, T.J. Jackson, who would soon go down in history as Stonewall, told his soldiers to "yell like furies," and just after 3:30 in the afternoon, the rebel yell rang out for the first time in the war. The Union soldiers, who had fought so well, faltered in the face of this screaming assault, and their retreat quickly lapsed into outright panic — many of them throwing down their weapons as they ran.

"They left artillery, small arms, muskets, rifles,

coats, blankets, provisions and everything," wrote Franklin Gaillard.

When the chase was over, and the enemy had reached the other side of the Potomac, Franklin returned to the original battlefield, where the reality of the war was suddenly all around him. Men lay dying in every part of the field, many of them groaning and begging for water. Numb at first, Franklin began gathering canteens from the dead, lifting the first, which was covered in blood, and pouring the contents gingerly into his own. After quenching his thirst, he made his rounds among the men still alive, tending first to those in gray, then giving water to his enemies as well.

"They seemed very grateful," he wrote to his father, "and were surprised at our kindness."

Franklin was convinced in that moment of victory that the war itself would soon be over. But his father in Mobile was not so sure. Things were not going as well in the west, where large rivers cut a path to the Confederate heartland. The Mississippi in the south and the Cumberland and Tennessee in the north all created easy routes for invasion, and by early 1862, the pressure was beginning to build from both ends. On February 16, the troops of Gen. Grant captured Fort Donelson on the border of Tennessee and Kentucky, and quickly pushed south all the way to Mississippi. Two months later, New Orleans fell to Admiral Farragut's fleet, which then steamed north toward the city of Vicksburg.

Thomas knew in his heart that the Confederacy was doomed. He was still in Mobile, barely 100 miles from the fighting, where he was waiting for the news and writing fatalistic predictions to his family. "The contest is fast approaching a crisis," he concluded in April, "and I am not sorry for it. The sooner it is brought to an issue the better....Let His will be done...."

But the problem for Thomas was that his sons were still caught in the middle of the killing. Edmund was a doctor, which may have been the most gruesome assignment of all. The field hospitals on both sides were grim — overrun after battles with the wounded and the maimed, who groaned and begged for some kind of relief and screamed with the amputation of their limbs, which were tossed into piles at the side of the tent. Samuel, too, did his time as a surgeon, but he served first as a captain in the regular army, promoted after the bloody battle of Corinth. In the summer of 1863, he was wounded and captured in the siege of Vicksburg, and five days later, his brother, Richebourg, was captured as well. Franklin, meanwhile, was still fighting in the east — promoted to colonel after the defeat at Gettysburg — and all across the Confederate States of America the killing continued, as the death toll soared toward a quarter of a million.

"Oh, this terrible war!" wrote Thomas. "Who

can measure the troubles — the affliction — it has brought upon us all? It has pleased the Almighty to inflict upon us this severe chastisement — and it is our duty to submit in Christian spirit....We can not foresee His ultimate purpose in thus scourging our people with the direst of calamities. But even in the depth of our sorrow, we can also see a glimmering of mercy."

The letter, in a sense, was a reflection of his life, which ended a short time after he wrote it. Thomas died in Mobile on February 2, 1864, just a few weeks short of his 74th birthday. He had experienced his share of frustration and failure, but the members of his family didn't remember him for that. In the letters they exchanged immediately after his death, they wrote instead of his integrity and kindness, and a dignity that seemed unaffected by his trials.

The word of his passing reached Franklin on the battlefields of Tennessee. A few days later, he wrote several letters to his family back home, remarking on the fact that there was nothing "mean or little" about his father. In his mind, Franklin carried old pictures from the past — of Thomas kneeling in prayer with his Bible, mahogany-red with gold block letters and commentaries scrawled on nearly every page. As Franklin and other members of the family understood it, the image was at the heart of his father's personality — his Christian fatalism that saved him from despair, even in moments when he had to be discouraged.

It was clear that Thomas had lived through some heartache, but he was nevertheless grateful for the other times too, and for the wisdom he had done his best to pass on. There was a symmetry, somehow, in the great movement of life, and even if a man couldn't always see it, it gave him a calmness to know that it was there.

Samuel Septimus Gaillard

Chapter 6
Reconstruction and Beyond

By the spring of 1864, the Civil War had entered a desperate stage. The previous year had not been a good one, even with the success of Lee's army in Virginia. With the fall of Vicksburg on July 4, and then Port Hudson a few days later, the Mississippi River now belonged to the North, and the situation seemed to be crumbling from there. Lee had pushed north into Pennsylvania, but had been driven back after the battle of Gettysburg, and now in Virginia in 1864, he was waiting for the invasion that he expected any day. His opponent this time was Gen. U.S. Grant, architect of the Union successes on the western front, recently handpicked by Abraham Lincoln to destroy Lee's army once and for all.

Lee, however, had other ideas. He knew that the war would be decided this year, and that the South, in fact, was down to one hope. If they could smash the army of Gen. Grant, inflicting enough casualties to drive it bleeding across the river into Maryland, perhaps it could damage Lincoln's chance of reelection. The voting that fall was almost certain to be a referendum on the war, and if things were going badly enough at the time, then maybe a peace candidate would emerge from the shadows and agree to acknowledge the independence of the South.

That was it. There was no other hope, for if Lincoln was elected for another four years, he had made it clear from his performance so far that he would continue the war for as long as it took — and time was not on the side of the South. Robert E. Lee understood all of this, and in May of 1864, he was waiting for Grant in the tangled wood thickets of northern Virginia, preparing to launch an all-out attack on an army nearly twice the size of his own.

Franklin Gaillard was ready for the fight. His unit had been moved north from Tennessee, and he was glad to be serving under Lee once again. He had been with him at Fredericksburg, Gettysburg and Chancellorsville — all of them as bloody as they were heroic, but Lee was a fighter and that's what it took. It was true that the battles were never routine, but after awhile a certain hardness set in, a belief in your own ability to survive that defied any rational calculation of the odds. It was that way in May in northern Virginia, as Lee's men waited in a place called the Wilderness. They were in good spirits, knowing that the terrain was on their side. It was a jungle almost — a tangled mass of scrub oaks and briers, with three main roads that tunneled through it and visibility so bad that an army of invaders couldn't see where to shoot. The problem was, neither could the forces of Gen. Lee, and when the battle began on May 5, the mayhem engulfed everyone who was in it. Men died by the hundreds in the first few hours, and many of the wounded were burned alive when the woods caught fire from the explosion of artillery and the flames spread faster than they were able to crawl.

When the nightmare continued at dawn the second day, Franklin Gaillard charged in again. He was a veteran now of a dozen other battles, promoted to colonel because of his bravery, and for nearly three years he had survived without a scratch. This time, however, his luck ran out. The bullet struck him early in the day, and the men around him knew it was serious. They dragged him to the rear, where, unable to speak, he quickly sank into unconsciousness and died. When word reached his relatives at home in Alabama, his sister, Lydia, pulled out a letter she had received in the winter. It was Franklin's last, written on the occasion of the death of their father — now made even sadder by the latest piece of news. "My dear brother..." she scribbled on the bottom.

But Franklin died in a winning cause, or at least it should have been. Badly outflanked and outmaneuvered, Grant lost 17,000 of his men — more than twice the losses that were suffered by Lee. Any other commander would have pulled back in defeat. McDowell, McClellan — they all seemed to know when it was time to retreat. But Gen. Grant kept coming. "Whatever happens," he had written to Lincoln, "there will be no turning back." And he was true to his promise — for five more weeks of the bloodiest fighting in the war, when his casualties soared to more than 60,000 men.

Lee had never seen anything like it, this war of attrition so vicious and bloody and this Yankee general who didn't seem to mind. Militarily, it made some sense. Grant could afford more losses than Lee. But it remained to be seen how it would play in the election — these endless days of stalemate fighting, with more and more families being touched by the killing.

What the North needed now was a lopsided success, and it finally came in the dog days of summer — on a hot August morning off the coast of Alabama. Admiral David Farragut, who had captured New Orleans and steamed with his fleet up the Mississippi River, now set his sights on the port of Mobile. It was one of the few that the Confederacy had left, and it had long been a haven for the blockade runners who helped keep the Southern states in the war. Farragut intended to change all that, though he knew the task would not be easy. Mobile was at the northern end of a bay, a body of water nearly 30 miles long, but narrow at the mouth. Fort Morgan and Fort Gaines, brick pentagons with a menacing array of 56 guns, guarded that mouth, and three rows of mines had been laid across the channel. But the mines were corroded by their long exposure to the salt, and most of them floated inert beneath the surface, as Farragut issued his now famous command — "Damn the torpedos, full speed ahead!" He lost one ship, but his others destroyed the Confederate fleet and sailed triumphant into the harbor.

It was a major military victory for the North, and psychologically it was critical, coming three months before the presidential election. Lincoln won, with a mandate now to finish the war, and his generals were well on their way to that goal. Grant was pushing deeper into Virginia, and Sherman was marching across Georgia to the sea. In desperation, Jefferson Davis, who had denounced Lincoln's Emancipation Proclamation, now decided to issue one of his own. He sent messengers to the governments of England and France, offering freedom for the slaves in exchange for recognition of the Confederacy. But the Europeans said no, and with the last hope gone, the war now limped to its painful conclusion. On April 9,

Lee surrendered his army at Appomattox, and the final mop-up work began.

At Fort Blakely in the swamps just north of Mobile, Samuel Gaillard was awaiting the end. His younger brother, Franklin, was already dead, and Richebourg, his older, now languished in a prison camp in Ohio, wondering at his fate. "We were taken without firing a shot," he had written of his capture. "If we were sacrificed for the good of the Army at Corinth, all well; but if we were neglected by our superiors with no such purpose, then there is nothing to console us." Samuel, meanwhile, had survived his wounds at the battle of Vicksburg and his ordeal as a prisoner before he was exchanged. But now it was about to happen again. On the day of Robert E. Lee's surrender, federal troops overran the stockade at Fort Blakely, and Sam was captured and taken away to Ship Island, a spit of sand off the coast of Mississippi.

It was a desolate place, with clusters of twisted oaks and pines and sand dunes bleached to the color of bone. Near the western end was a wooden stockade with a handful of wooden huts inside. It was a miserable confinement for the Blakely survivors. They knew by now that the war was lost, with Lee defeated and the Confederate cabinet in flight across the South. But there was a final indignity that they hadn't counted on. The Ship Island prisoners were entrusted to the charge of Negro troops, and Sam later told the members of his family that it was the most humiliating moment of his life. The guards, still angry at their own servitude, were seldom sympathetic to these Confederate rebels, who had gone to war for the right to own slaves. As Sam remembered it, the prisoners were cursed and prodded with bayonets, and a few were even shot when they moved too slow. It was a reminder, he said, of just how bitter their defeat was going to be.

Sam came home to Monroe County, looking gaunt and tired, with his angular face more sunken than usual and his goatee now showing flecks of gray. He knew that they faced an uncertain future, and it was becoming clear already that John Wilkes Booth hadn't done them any favors when he murdered their old arch-enemy, Mr. Lincoln. The irony of it was difficult to bear. The South had nursed such a hatred for Lincoln, but in the final months of the war, the president had been the voice of reconciliation — making speeches about the need to put the country back together "with malice toward none, and charity for all." Now with his death, other voices were emerging. One of those belonged to Thaddeus Stevens, a Pennsylvania congressman who regarded the South as a "conquered province" and most of the former rebels as "traitors." Stevens was a formidable presence in Washington — a craggy-faced man with dark eyebrows, a piercing stare, and a gift for expressing himself in debate. His invective provided the salt for open wounds, and the Gaillards viewed him with hatred and fear, remembering well into the 20th century "the spirit of Thaddeus Stevens...with all its humiliation and tragedy."

There were reasons for the family to feel that way. By anybody's standards, Stevens was a shrill and uncompromising man — the primary proponent of military reconstruction, who believed that the South should be punished for its sins. Some people said his demand for retribution was prompted in part by the destruction of his iron works business in Pennsylvania by the invading army of Robert E. Lee. But his reasons, in fact, went deeper than that, for Stevens was a man of passionate conviction. He grew up poor in northern Vermont and championed the cause of the country's have-nots, particularly the blacks, long before there was any political advantage in the stance. As a lawyer in the years before the Civil War, he was a frequent defender of runaway slaves, never charging his clients for that service, and as a member of congress he opposed the spread of slavery to the territories. Stevens saw in the Civil War a golden opportunity, not only to eradicate the institution of slavery, but to secure for blacks the same civil rights that were accorded to whites — including, at a minimum, the right to vote.

He was opposed in that by Andrew Johnson,

Abraham Lincoln's successor in the White House, who had little sympathy for the former slaves. He vetoed a bill to grant them civil rights and pronounced them inherently unfit for the vote. In one of the most astonishing statements ever issued by a President of the United States, Johnson insisted that blacks in general "have shown a constant tendency to relapse into barbarism," and that as a result of their congenital failing as a race, "White men alone must manage the South."

Stevens was appalled by the president's example and the laws that were passed in response by the South. Mississippi and South Carolina were the worst, but all over the region, whites enacted measures denying blacks the right to vote, hold office, sue a white man or serve on a jury; to speak disrespectfully or even to stand idle when there was work to be done in a white man's field. To many people in the North, the rebels who enacted such hideous legislation demonstrated, at best, a startling lack of contrition. In the backlash that followed, Stevens and his radical colleagues in congress pushed through a sweeping series of measures granting black Americans the right to vote and to stand as equals in the eyes of the law. They also sent federal troops to the South to assure at the point of a bayonet if necessary that whites would adjust to the new social order.

For blacks, it was the answer to generations of prayer, a time when they could finally step forward unafraid, and many of them firmly assumed their places in a world that suddenly was so full of hope. Hiram Revels, for example, was a teacher from Fayetteville, N.C., who moved to Mississippi and won a seat in the senate — a position last held by Jefferson Davis. Fifteen other blacks served in the congress, another was governor of Louisiana, and hundreds more rose to lesser positions, ranging from sheriff to justice of the peace.

If it seemed that the day of justice had dawned, whites in the South saw a different reality — the confusion of a world turned upside down. Among the Gaillards, their discomfort at the power of the former slaves was heightened by fears for their own social standing. Sam, for example, had quietly resumed his practice as a doctor, rumbling through the hills of Monroe County, only to discover that many of his patients couldn't pay. The cotton economy was now in shambles, and he could see the results among the members of his family.

His sister-in-law, Caroline, widow of his older brother, John, had six children still living at home and was nearly destitute by the end of the war. In a way, she could blame nobody but herself. Early in 1865, she had decided to sell off her handful of slaves, while buyers for them could still be found. But when auction day came, she had second thoughts. The first slave on the block, an aging house servant by the name of Hannah, wept softly at the sound of the auctioneer's voice. Perhaps it was simply the indignity of the moment, or her fear that she might be torn from her children, or perhaps it was partly what her mistress assumed — that Hannah was grieving at her separation from the Gaillards. Whatever the case, Caroline abruptly called off the sale, and the poverty she faced at the end of the war was simply a confirmation of her pride. Sometimes a person had to do what was right.

But the times were hard in southern Alabama, and the unaccustomed pain of now being poor was heightened by the rhetoric cascading from the North, the gloating from the radicals like Thaddeus Stevens, and the occupying army that had removed the South's chosen leaders from office and enforced the beginnings of a whole new society. In South Carolina, for example, Sam Gaillard's cousin, Peter Charles, was summarily overthrown as mayor of Charleston. The pattern was repeated all across the South, and within a few years the anger of whites was turning once again to a cry for blood.

In Sumter County, Ala., near the Mississippi line, a black legislator named Richard Burke was murdered by whites who considered him extreme. In that same autumn of 1870, the Ku Klux Klan broke up a rally further north in Greene County, killing four blacks and wounding 54. The western part of the state was the worst, but when blacks began to flee across the line to Mississippi, they found more violence waiting for them there. In Meridian in March of 1871, whites set out on a murderous spree, killing 30 black people in a single day — including nearly all of the city's black leaders.

The violence grew worse as the century progressed. By the 1890s, Negroes were being lynched in the South at the rate of two a week, and the pace didn't slacken for more than a decade. These were sometimes the most grisly executions, with torture and mutilation preceding the deaths, and the killers posing for pictures with their victims. Race riots, too, were a common occurrence, with the worst coming in Atlanta, New Orleans and Wilmington, N.C. White mobs roamed the streets, shooting down any Negro they could find.

Many whites, of course, didn't approve of the violence, but most heartily approved of the result, which was to restore the South as a white man's country. By the end of the century, the terror had been buttressed by the force of law, with blacks segregated and stripped of the vote and reduced to a status that was officially second class. The Gaillards simply saw it as normal.

"Touch the white race when or where you can," one of them wrote, "and you find a race of progress stamping itself upon the civilization of the ages. Touch the black race when or where you can, throughout the unnumbered ages, and you find a race so far below the one that could conceive great things and build cities and towers that reached toward the skies....

"Like draws to like, and birds of a feather will forever flock together...."

As the world in the South was being made right, the Gaillards went about the restoration of the family. Sam continued his work as a doctor, working side by side with his youngest son, Walter — a gentle physician whose bedside manner, in the words of one patient, "was a tonic in itself." His oldest son, Frye, became a farmer, a robust man who worked the soil and lived to the age of 98, sipping his share of good whiskey in the evenings.

Palmer, meanwhile, moved south to Mobile. He was the second of Sam's three sons, and maybe the most ambitious of the group — a handsome young man, slender and erect, with an angular face, flashing brown eyes, and a wave near the part of his neatly combed hair. He decided to embark on the study of law, following a pattern now common in the South — a drift from the land and the life of a planter toward a profession less threatened by changes in the weather. There was a stability, somehow, in the practice of law, and on July 5, 1881, Palmer took his place as a member of the bar.

A few years later, his mentor, Peter Hamilton, gave him a book — a handsome biography of

Ralph Waldo Emerson, written by Oliver Wendell Holmes. Palmer thumbed through it to page 183 and marked a passage not far from the top. "Character," wrote Emerson in one of his essays, "is nature in its highest form." Palmer already was fascinated by the subject. As he entered his 30s, he had no way of knowing that he would one day emerge as the next great patriarch of the family, perhaps the last. But he was intrigued by those who had gone before — Peter and Thomas and the others down the line — and he hoped someday to be worthy of their example.

But in the meantime, he was still a young man, with other things on his mind. At the top of the list was his discovery in 1892 that he had fallen in love.

Her name was Maddie, and he knew that he had to have her as his wife.

Palmer Gaillard and his bride, Maddie

Chapter 7
The Last Patriarch

The engagement year was not an easy one for them. Maddie Wilson had gone to New York to study at a conservatory of music, and it was a painful separation from there to Mobile, where Palmer was struggling to establish his career. The days were long and the nights were lonely, but he did his best to bear it with grace. He was nearly 36 and deeply in love with this dark-haired girl, who was only now in her 22nd year. He admired her talent — her voice so full of sweetness and strength, which were the qualities that he also saw in her character. But Palmer was uncertain about a date for the wedding, wondering about his own ability to provide.

Maddie came from a prominent family, one of

the richest in all of Mobile, with an estate so grand it took his breath. There were oak trees leading to the antebellum house — a canopy that rustled with the streams of Spanish moss, and gardens of roses and azaleas everywhere. The grounds were the passion of Maddie's grandfather, Lorenzo Madison Wilson, a Mobile banker and railroad magnate, and his wife, Augusta Evans, who had emerged as one of the country's leading authors. The critics were invariably hard on her novels, Victorian love stories, dripping with moralism and propriety, and a style that many writers saw as pretentious — "affectation run mad," as one contemporary put it. But Augusta was consoled by the response of the public, who bought her books in unprecedented numbers, adding still more to the family estate.

Maddie was raised in this environment, coming to live at her grandparents' home — Ashland Place, it was called — when she was not yet one. Her father was killed soon after her birth, and it was, without any serious competition, the most stunning tragedy in the history of the family. On a July morning in 1871, Louis Wilson, the handsome son of Lorenzo, was shot to death on a Mobile street. Everyone knew the name of his assailant, for Braxton Bragg was one of the prominent men in the city, the son of a judge, and a nephew of the general for whom he was named. Braxton had been a critic of the Wilson family, charging that old-man Lorenzo, the principal stockholder of a streetcar line, was using its mules to plow his own fields. With the family honor thus affronted, Louis Wilson sprang to his father's defense. There was talk of a duel, for Louis was something of a hothead himself. He was 21 years old, a dashing young man with passion in his eyes, who promised that the family name would be avenged.

According to one story handed down through the years, Bragg threatened to kill him if he came into town, and Louis announced that he was coming anyway. Bragg was waiting, and true to his word, shot Louis dead as he disembarked from the train.

Some people said the whole episode was more ambiguous, with threats and counter threats flying everywhere, and the authorities decided that no charges were required. But on the morning of the funeral, Braxton Bragg watched from the balcony of his home as the somber procession passed below him on the street. He had been stationed by his father to take it all in, a penance for a killing that didn't have to be. And many years later, he confided more than once to Palmer Gaillard that he didn't know the meaning of a good night's sleep.

But life at Ashland Place moved on, and Maddie grew from a baby into young womanhood. She felt at home with the rhythms of the place and became accustomed to its elegance and wealth. But she also was impatient, during her year in New York, with Palmer's reluctance to set a date for their wedding. He could be so infuriating sometimes, his letters so reserved and unromantic, even if they were sprinkled with intelligence and wit. She complained about it in her own correspondence, wondering periodically at the depth of his love. His replies to those letters were more what she wanted — tender and reassuring, filled with his longing to hold her in his arms.

Finally, in 1893, she returned to Alabama and they were married. A child was born the following year, and by the turn of the century, they were on their way to five. Times were happy in the Gaillard family. They bought a new house in 1903, and it was precisely what Palmer was hoping to provide — a handsome place with six white columns and hand-carved doors of cypress. The ceilings inside were 16 feet — high enough for the hot air to rise and the cool gulf breezes to drift through the hallways.

It was a prestige address, about an hour by carriage from the heart of downtown, up a long sloping hill just west of the city, where the rich built houses to escape the yellow fever, a terrible plague to the people of Mobile. The disease descended on the city every couple of years, bringing high fever and a racking cough, striking mostly at night — as if it were somehow carried on the mist. By the turn of the century, it was beginning to disappear, but Spring Hill had remained a sanctuary from the fever. The Gaillards were proud of their cultured, five-acre retreat. Palmer had seen the house of his grandfather, Thomas, and he had read the earliest descriptions of the Rocks, the ancestral homeplace of Capt. Peter Gaillard. The family had never been a stranger to beauty, and Palmer was happy to carry on that tradition, with his flower gardens blooming every season of the year. He could see that Maddie was happy, too, taking her greatest delight in the children.

It was hard to believe when her health began to fail. Tuberculosis hit her in her early 30s, and it kept getting worse. Palmer sent her for a while to a drier climate, but she missed her children and decided to return. When she died in the fall of 1907, he put her jewelry in a small envelope, and penned a stoic notation on the front: "Engagement & wedding rings of my wife. She died Nov. 11, '07 at 3:50 am."

There seemed to be nothing else to say.

Palmer moved on with the other parts of his life. He and Maddie had been together for 14 years, and even at the terrible moment of her death, he could feel a gratitude for her life.

He was now in his 50s and beginning to emerge as one of the most prominent lawyers in the state — prominent enough to receive an invitation when the President of the United States came to town. It was easy to be impressed with Woodrow Wilson.

He was the first Southern-born president since the Civil War — proof of the South's restoration to the Union. He was also a contemporary of Palmer Gaillard's, born in the same year, carrying the same childhood memories of the war — and very importantly to many people in the South, harboring similar views on the issue of race. He arranged for a private showing in the White House of the controversial film, *The Birth of a Nation*, extolling the virtues of white supremacy and the heroic interventions of the Ku Klux Klan. "Like writing history with lightning," Wilson said when it was over, and he also announced that it was "terribly true."

But on his trip to Mobile, Wilson's mind was less on the past than on the shape of the world in the century just beginning. He spoke of a new international order, an end to imperialism and aggression, with the American people now leading the way. "The United States," he declared, "will never again seek one additional foot of territory by conquest."

He was convincing when he said such things. He still had the aura of Princeton about him, that whiff of elegance and erudition that served to give his ideals greater force. It was hard to imagine on his visit to Mobile that his gentle rationality would be overwhelmed. But a crisis was building on the continent of Europe, and in less than a year it had spilled into war — a conflagration so terrible that everything before it merely seemed like practice. The difference in the world could be traced to one thing. In 1862, an American inventor named Richard J. Gatling, had applied for a patent on a new kind of gun. A "machine gun," he called it, and there was something ominous in the juxtaposition of the words. By the 1890s, his invention had been perfected. It could fire at the rate of 50 bullets a second — an astonishing feat that the generals, at first, didn't seem to comprehend. As the battle lines were drawn across Europe, the armies still feinted and charged at each other, just as armies had done in the past. This time, however, they were simply cut to pieces. On April 9, 1917, three days after the United States had entered the war, the British army under Douglas Haig launched an attack on the German lines and lost 160,000 men in one battle. It was a catastrophic moment in human history, serving in the minds of many Europeans to reverse the whole notion of human progress. How could things be getting any better when the civilized world had come to this?

Certainly, these horrors on the battlefields of France had destroyed the old notions of warfare itself — the ideas of gallantry, adventure and courage. The war was now an exercise in the mud, parallel trenches across the face of Europe, stretching from the coast of Belgium to the Alps. There was only one exception to the whole dreary pattern — a throwback of sorts to a different kind of fighting. In the skies above Flanders and northern France, the airplane made its entrance in the war, with daring pilots going one on one, testing the limits of their machinery and nerve.

One of these was Palmer Gaillard's son — Palmer Jr., the oldest of three, a swashbuckling boy of 21, skinny and intense, with jet black hair and a rakish sense of humor. He must have understood the odds, the possibilities of being shot from the sky, but it was better somehow than being killed in a ditch. Besides, it was clear that he was pretty good at it. He had three kills in the first few weeks, and the adventure was grand, like the stories of cavalry from the old Civil War. But then one morning he was drifting alone, his motor stalled above the enemy lines, with a squadron of Germans bearing down in a hurry. He dove through the clouds near the town of St. Mihiel, and crash-landed short of the American side. He lay for a day in no-man's land, in a bombed out crater halfway between the trenches.

The following morning, a telegram arrived in Mobile, informing Palmer Gaillard Sr. that his son was missing and probably dead. His plane had crashed and there was no sign of life.

There is no record of how Palmer reacted, or the memories that must have flooded his mind. Nor do we know his response when the second message came, telling him, in fact, that his son was alive. He had been thrown from the plane, and according to one account, had lain unconscious for more than a day before he awakened and cried out for help. When nightfall came, an American soldier crawled out to find him and dragged him back to the American lines. Remarkably enough, his injuries were minor, and after a few days rest, Palmer Jr. was back in the skies.

The armistice came on November 11, 1918, and as the statesmen hammered out the Treaty of Versailles, the Gaillards began to move on with their lives. Palmer Sr. was proud of his sons. Wilson was probably the steadiest of the three. He became a dentist soon after the war, as well as a conservationist and author. He roamed the woodlands of southern Alabama, hunting deer and wild turkey, and peering at the birds through his battered binoculars. Meanwhile, his two brothers, Palmer Jr. and Walter, went to work for their father. They built a successful law firm in Mobile, with Palmer Sr. the dean of his profession.

His major client was a jaunty politician by the name of Frank Boykin, a congressman who represented Mobile. Boykin was known as a wheeler-dealer, the kind of rough-and-tumble, old-school capitalist whose business dealings could keep a law firm afloat. He grew up poor in Washington County, just north of Mobile, and made his fortune as a land speculator. He bought up 150,000 acres of what appeared to be nothing but pine trees and briers, then built a sawmill and began selling turpentine and timber. Boykin was a man of irre-pressible good humor, and Palmer Gaillard loved him. They were nothing alike. Palmer was quiet, aristocratic and proper, while Boykin was a scrap-per, outrageous and vain. But he needed somebody to keep him out of trouble, and for nearly 50 years, Palmer did his best.

Palmer was 97 when he won his last case for Boykin, a dispute involving the turpentine com-pany. He prepared the written arguments himself as the case made its way to the Supreme Court of Alabama. The judges had never seen anything like it — 91 printed pages, citing verses from Genesis and the general principles of justice, but no case law at all. "The appellee's brief is certainly un-usual," one justice wrote in the unanimous opinion handed down by the court. "The writer...has fur-nished us with one of the most remarkable documents it has been our pleasure to peruse...."

By the 1950s, the accolades were routine for Palmer Gaillard, coming, it seemed, in every facet of his life. He was an old man now, fast emerging as an institution — an elder statesman in the life of Alabama, and a towering presence among the members of his family. Sometimes, in fact, he could be overwhelming. He lived with his daugh-ters in the house he had purchased in 1903, a gift to Maddie and their five children. Neither Mary nor Flora Gaillard had ever married, choosing instead to remain with their father. Flora certainly had had her chances. She lived for awhile in New York City and had suitors there, which was not surprising. She was pretty enough to work as a model, and she must have been impressed with life in the cultural center of the country — the gaiety of it, and the intellectual zest. Flora was the oldest of the Gaillard siblings, and some people said she was also the brightest. She did well enough at Agnes Scott, then took her degree at Columbia University. She decided, however, to return to Mobile, and it was apparently a wrenching separation from her boyfriends.

"Dear Flora," one of them wrote, "I'm sorry it was to end like this, causing such anguish, but you were the one who refused to leave your father and the house. Forgive me...."

In the end her motivations were a mystery. Was there unspoken pressure from the old man himself, telling her without ever using the words that he wanted her to give up her life for his? Or did he simply allow her to do it? Flora never said. She seldom spoke of her New York days, or the things that might have been, settling instead into a life of routine. At 8 every morning for the next fifty years, she made the one-block walk out the back gate of her house and up the narrow dirt lane to the schoolhouse. She was a third-grade teacher, dedicated and stern, and her beauty was now replaced with something else — a ferocious primness, some people said, that left her raging at the changes all around her. Her greatest nightmare was the civil rights movement, especially after September of 1957, when the president sent his soldiers to Little Rock, Ark., to oversee the desegregation of the schools. Flora had no sympathy for Elizabeth Eckford and the eight other black students who were threatened by the mobs outside of Central High. She remembered instead her father's bitter stories of Reconstruction and the changes enforced by an occupying army. Little Rock seemed like a *deja vu.*

She vowed it wouldn't happen in her classroom. If they sent any Negro third-graders to her, she would assign them to seats in the back of the room and never acknowledge their presence again. Sadly enough, the people who knew her understood that she meant it.

Mary was different. As the youngest in the family, she was softer somehow — not as pretty as her sister, though she held her own with her small round face and dangling curls. Later in life, she was short and plump and fond of puttering in the five-acre yard. She, too, was given to outbursts of temper, which subsided as abruptly and unpredictably as they came — and like Flora and her father, she was a fountain of stories about the Gaillard family, a keeper of the myth. Her versions, in fact, were probably the best, for she seemed to have no fear of embellishment. There were tales of Reconstruction and the Civil War, the American

Revolution and the Southern frontier. Every account, of course, had a Gaillard hero, for as Mary understood it, the family honor had been steeled in the past — a nobility that only a Southerner could understand.

As she entered middle age, the family had emerged as the great love of her life — not so much the individuals who comprised it, for they were venerated, tolerated or despised, depending on which of her emotions they had earned. But their common ancestry was something to revere. It was a lesson she had learned from her patriarch father, and they spent many hours on the family genealogy — updating, refining, adding bits of commentary to the story.

They also worked to keep up the homeplace, which was now at the center of the family universe. The Big House itself had never looked better, with its gleaming white columns, rocking chairs on the porch, and grounds that were also stately and fine. There were grassy avenues leading in from the road, shaded by magnolias and live oak trees, and bamboo hedges growing down by the garden. A grape arbor formed a green shelter every spring, surrounded by the stands of pear trees and figs, with the scent of sweet wisteria in the woods. Mary Gaillard was the master of it all. She tended the grounds in the company of her father, who relished the exercise at the age of 95, and a gentle black man named Robert Croshon, who had worked for the Gaillards for most of his life. Robert seemed to enjoy his calling well enough, finding his peace and satisfaction in the soil, and if the pay was meager — $14 a week when he started — he nevertheless felt a kinship with the family. They had come to Mobile at the same time as his own, though the circumstances, of course, were not the same.

Robert's ancestors were runaway slaves. They had left their Georgia plantation one night, expecting to follow the Drinking Gourd north. But the Big Dipper was obscured by a sudden thunderstorm, and in the confusion they found themselves headed south. The escape was led by Gilbert Fields, Robert's great-grandfather. Gilbert was an African, apparently a proud and restless man, who fled with his wife, two daughters and a grandchild. One daughter was lost in the frantic escape and never heard from again. But the others found a cave, probably somewhere near the Alabama line, where another runaway had built a house underground. He took them in and fed them, told them they could stay, but they decided to keep pushing south to Mobile, which in a way, was the next best thing to the North. The city was a haven for free Negroes. There were more than 1,000 in 1850, which was half the total for the state of Alabama. Their lives weren't easy. They had to report once a year to renew their papers, and it was a crime for them to congregate on the downtown streets or use "insulting" language toward whites. It was better, however, than being a slave, and Gilbert Fields found work at a church.

A half century later, his granddaughter Rachel, the child he had carried to freedom in the storm, became a cook for the Gaillard family. Her days often lasted for 15 hours, starting with breakfast at 6 a.m. — bacon and eggs, with grits and hot biscuits — then a midday meal for whoever was at home and another full dinner at 6 in the evening. Robert Croshon was Rachel's young cousin, and he soon began working for the Gaillards, too. By the 1950s, he was a fixture on the place, working with Palmer in his garden, tilling the soil and putting in the seeds, beating back the invasions of insects and weeds. He knew the old man was a white supremacist, convinced of the superiority of his race, but to Robert at least, it didn't show in his manner. In fact, the old man was kind. There were many days when the chores were all done and they would sit together beside the rows of collards, the big-headed kind that grew knee-high, and they would talk about anything that came to mind — their families maybe, or the garden, or God.

"Robert," the old man told him more than once, speaking gravely in his deep baritone, almost as if he were delivering a speech, "you've been blessed with good ability. Don't let anybody think they are better."

Many years later, Robert told the story with

appreciation and smiled as others came flooding to his mind.

"We'd be working hard in the garden," he remembered, "and I'd be pushing that hand plow fast. Mr. Gaillard would say, 'Robert, take your time. You get there even if you don't hurry.'

"Another time, he asked me if I went to church. I said, 'Yes sir.' He said, 'Good. I don't think much of a man who doesn't go to church.'"

Through all of those years, and all the hard work and conversations, there was never any doubt about who was in charge. But the two of them sweated side by side, and Robert regarded the old man with affection.

"He was," he concluded, "a good, kind man."

The 1950s, however, were a troubled time in Alabama. Black Americans came home from World War II, having done their part in the fight against tyranny, and they expected a little more freedom for themselves. They had some allies now. When a group of black citizens in South Carolina, not far from the ancestral home of the Gaillards, went to court in the pursuit of better schools, they found some judges who were willing to listen. They asked for an end to segregated schools, and in 1954, having considered their case and four others like it, the U.S. Supreme Court ruled in their favor.

Palmer Gaillard understood the stakes, especially after 1955, when the contagion of hope

106

among black Americans spread to Alabama, and a stubborn black woman named Rosa Parks refused to relinquish her seat on a bus. As Palmer saw clearly, the issue was not the bus system of Montgomery, or even the survival of segregated schools. This was an assault on the whole social order, much like the one he had seen in his youth. Palmer, once again, was determined to resist it. At the astonishing age of 102, he wrote an article for the journal of the Alabama Bar Association, decrying "the spirit of Thaddeus Stevens [which] may force upon us a second Reconstruction...."

He also raised the issue in his church, a forum he regarded as even more important. Palmer was known as a man of deep faith. Every night in the Big House, precisely at 9, he would take his place in the rocking chair by the hearth and thumb through the well-worn pages of his Bible, selecting the verses to be read aloud. The psalms were his favorites, those bits of poetry that were written by kings, but there were others also that were scattered through the Book — the words of the prophets and the Sermon on the Mount.

Palmer was an elder in the Presbyterian church, an office he had held for 65 years. But now in the final decade of his life there were troubling new divisions among the members of his church. Their minister, John Crowell, was a learned young man of stunning eloquence, with the kindest heart the old man had ever seen. But he was one of a handful of Mobile ministers who preached a few sermons on the issue of race — calling essentially for an end to segregation. Palmer Gaillard didn't agree. He had grown accustomed to the Southern way of life, which seemed to resemble what God had intended, and many of his fellow church members concurred. And yet they were drawn to this brilliant young preacher, with his spell-binding words and a faith that was clearly a match for their own.

It was a dilemma that Palmer helped settle with grace. He made his own position known, writing a letter to the elders "with the prayer that my church and yours may be spared the results of...integration." He recalled his days as a Sunday School teacher at a church of former slaves and expressed his pride that in the course of his long career as a lawyer, he had never lost a case "in representing a negro against a white man." But he also expressed his deepening fear that in the South and elsewhere, "a unity of Spirit is endangered in an effort to bring about a unity of the Flesh."

He understood that John Crowell disagreed. The minister regarded segregation as wrong — a patent affront to the dignity of black Americans — and the two of them argued about it some. Their disagreements, however, were civil and discreet. In public, to Crowell's everlasting amazement, the old man chose to back him every time.

Perhaps the most basic issue they faced was what to do on Sunday if a black person came to worship at the church. Would he be made welcome — or, as some in the congregation suggested, turned away in deference to the Southern way of life? To Crowell, of course, the answer was clear, but his stance drew fire from some people in the church, until the day the old man rose to speak. He was an amazing figure at the age of 99, nearly 6-feet-1, if a little bit stooped, with clothes that were beginning to sag on his frame. But his voice was strong, as he cleared his throat and proclaimed once again that the minister was right. Even in the days of his ancestors, he said, slaves had been allowed to worship in the balconies. Surely today, they would not retreat from the wisdom and generosity of their fathers. But more than that, they should also remember that "our Lord looks not on the color of skin, but on the quality of a man's heart and his character and soul."

It was a powerful performance, as it usually was when the old man spoke — as if his words, somehow, should be inscribed on a tablet. And yet it left John Crowell perplexed. This was clearly a man of integrity, and the leap was so small from his professions of faith to a support for the end of segregation in the South. But Palmer Gaillard resisted that connection. Kindness was one thing, equality quite another, and he continued writing letters for the rest of his life, arguing that integration was a threat to both races — especially his own. He and John Crowell continued to debate it, with no trace of progress, until the day in 1959 when Crowell got word that the old man was dying.

It was a day he had dreaded for more than a decade — the end of a life so spirited and grand — and he drove out quickly to the house in Spring Hill. Palmer was now 103, and he looked so fragile as he lay in the bed, his breathing shallow and his skin ghost-white. He couldn't have weighed more than a hundred pounds, and his voice when he spoke was barely a whisper. The preacher took a seat on the side of the bed and the old man slowly reached out his hand.

"Pastor..." he whispered, letting the word hang there as he gathered his breath. "I must tell you now, I see now that you were right."

There were just the two of them in the half-darkened room, where the shadows fell softly on the old man's bed. He didn't say anything after that, just shut his eyes as the preacher held his hand. The next morning he was gone.

As the 1950s drew to a close, John Crowell thought often about that confession, and it somehow gave him a reason to hope. Palmer Gaillard was such a symbol of the South. He had lived through more than half of its history, if you began counting time with the founding of the country, and he had seen everything since the great Civil War — the temporary upheavals of Reconstruction, and the eventual restoration of his family and his race. He was proud of the legacy he had sought to pass on — that code of honor and generosity and kindness, but in the clarity of those final moments of his life, he may have understood that it wasn't enough.

John Crowell thought so. And the question now for the American South — confronted with the darker implications of its past — was whether those still living could understand it as well.

The Big House

Frye Gaillard

Chapter 8
Listening to the Elders

I remember it simply as a warm, sunny day, though it must have been fall, for leaf piles were burning, the sweet scent drifting through the neighborhood. Robert Croshon was there with his wheelbarrow, and I was five years old and ready for a ride. It was something of a ritual for us by now. Every Saturday on his way to work, Robert would stop to pick up his "helper." That was me — the youngest and most favored of Palmer Gaillard's grandchildren.

The old man was 90 by the time I was born, still full of vigor, though I remember his deafness, the deep wrinkles in his face, and the wispy white hair that tousled in the breeze. I called him Dad, the name permitted to anyone in the family, and I loved those hours that we spent together — just he and Robert and I in the garden. Robert was a man of great dignity and patience, hard-working and quiet, with a reassuring face, a broad, flat nose, gentle eyes, and a voice that was rich and resonant and kind.

He and Dad worked hard and steady, while I practiced high-jumping across the rows of collard greens and chased away the Indians in the bamboo hedges. On one of those mornings in the 1950s, we broke for lunch around the middle of the day. The spread was impressive — fried chicken, greens, homegrown tomatoes, a platter of hot biscuits — covering every inch of the dining room table. But as we took our places around the great cluttered feast, Robert found a chair at the table in the kitchen.

To a five-year-old, it made no sense. "Robert!" I called, "come on in here."

I knew immediately that I had made a mistake. The silence was sudden, and my Aunt Mary shot me a look that could kill. "Shame on you," she said with a hiss. "Shame on you for hurting Robert's feelings."

There were many different lessons contained in that moment – the most important of which was that however silly the world might appear, there were just certain subjects that we didn't talk about. Actually, it was easy enough to avoid them, for the diversions were plentiful for a boy growing up in

Mobile. There were baseball cards to be traded in the summer and great limbs that beckoned from the live oak trees, some of them broad enough to walk. But the most passionate diversion was reserved for September, the date set aside for the beginning of football. We lived, of course, in the country of the Bear — Paul "Bear" Bryant, the football coach at the University of Alabama, who restored the fortunes of a losing program and became the biggest hero in the state.

There was something magical from the moment he arrived. He won five games in 1958, and three years later, a national championship — the first of five before he was through. He prowled the sidelines in his hounds-tooth cap, growling at everybody who came within range, and his mumbling mystique was Southern to the bone. He was humble in victory, gracious in defeat, praising his players whenever they won, and blaming nobody but himself when they lost. The boys on the team were a lot like he was. They played the game hard and mostly clean, never argued with officials or got into fights, and of course they almost always won. That was important in the state of Alabama, where winning was otherwise uncommon. We felt a little like the national stepchild — 49th most years in what we spent for education, and sometimes lower in a few other categories. In addition to that, there was a revolution underway, and a great many of us, by the end of the '50s, were not

115

at all sure we were on the winning side.

As far as we could tell, it began up the road in the city of Montgomery, this relentless intrusion of the outside world, compelling us to think about things that seemed better left alone. On December 5, 1955, a young black preacher named Martin Luther King, 26-years-old and fresh out of graduate school in Boston, made a speech to a rally at a Montgomery church. We had no way of knowing when we first heard about it that, in the late afternoon before the speech, King was so overwhelmed by his doubts — his sense of inadequacy for the task that lay ahead — that he put his trembling pen aside and prayed that God would help him find the words. Such images were invisible to white Alabamians. What we saw instead was an insurrection, reaching far beyond the modest demands of the moment: courtesy on the part of white bus drivers, and a policy of first-come, first-serve seating — with blacks still filling the buses from the rear.

Imbedded in the majestic sweep of King's sermon were intimations of a shredded status quo — a radical recasting of the Southern way of life, with blacks leading the way on the road to redemption. And the most disconcerting thing was this: Despite his secret fears on that same afternoon, Martin Luther King seemed to be so sure. "We are not wrong tonight," he proclaimed, as the amens swelled and filled up the church. "If we are wrong, the Supreme Court of this nation is wrong. If we are wrong, the Constitution of the United States is wrong. If we are wrong, God Almighty is wrong....If we are wrong, justice is a lie."

I still remember the response of my family — the rage at the impudence of this middle-class Negro, who may have been raised in the state of Georgia, but picked up some funny ideas in Boston. As a child I didn't know what to think, though I did know better than to talk about it much. But then I saw him one day in Birmingham. It was seven years later, and I had come to the city on a high school trip. King was there as the civil rights movement was rushing toward a peak. He was afraid of Birmingham. He thought it was a place where he might be killed, for this was the city of Eugene "Bull" Connor, the infamous Commissioner of Public Safety who regarded brutality as a necessary tool. But for the civil rights movement, that was the point. King and the others intended to show that segregation in the South had never been benign — that it was not simply custom, or polite separation (as the Gaillard family, among others, liked to claim), but rather an ugly and violent stain, immoral at its core. They hoped that Bull Connor would not disappoint them.

The skirmishing began in April of 1963, just before Easter Sunday. I happened to be there as King was arrested, and at the moment it didn't seem particularly historic. The crowd of marchers was small, no more than 50, and by the time I wandered onto the scene, it was almost over. Somebody told me there had been some demonstrations at a lunch counter, and then the march, but the police now had it under control. They were hauling King away to a paddy wagon, and even to the whites who had learned to hate him, he didn't seem especially threatening anymore. He was a smallish man in blue overalls, with an expression that betrayed neither anger nor fear but a stoicism that seemed to shade into sadness.

The sympathy I felt for him came in a flash, almost involuntary at first. I don't remember thinking of segregation or civil rights but simply that I knew who the underdog was — the victim of a cruelty that grew more vivid in the next few days, as the snarling Bull Connor turned loose his dogs and aimed his fire hoses at the crowds of demonstrators. It was not always that simple and pat, for there were blacks who showered the policemen with rocks. But Connor and his troopers made no distinction between those who were violent and those who were not. The images flashing across the country were awful — German Shepherds tearing at a teenager's flesh, while another was knocked from his feet by a hose and blown along the ground like a piece of tissue paper.

It was exactly what Martin Luther King had hoped for — a demonstration of the violence at the heart of segregation — and yet he brooded about it in private. People were getting hurt out there in the streets, and some of them were barely more than children. The citizens of Birmingham blamed him for it, the white ones at least. Even the most moderate ministers in the city issued a statement condemning the protests, charging that King's non-violence was a mockery, for violence, after all, was precisely the point — the drama that kept the movement in the headlines.

King recognized the grain of truth, especially in September, when dynamite exploded at a Birmingham church. It was 10:29 on a Sunday morning, and the crowds were beginning to gather for worship. Four teenaged girls — Carol Robertson, Addie Mae Collins, Cynthia Wesley and Denise McNair — were especially excited on this particular morning, a balmy and peaceful later -summer's day, with the sound of church bells and the singing of birds. They and other junior high students were invited to participate in the service for adults. They had gone to the ground-floor rest-room to primp, when the bomb went off and ripped through the wall — killing all four in a cascade of bricks. A civil defense team dug through the rubble, finding bits of clothing and a patent leather shoe before they came to the bodies. King was in Atlanta when the phone call came, bringing with it all the grisly details — four murdered girls, who were killed for one reason: Their church had been a base of operations for his movement.

The members of his family had never seen him so depressed.

This was segregation laid bare, but he had never quite dreamed that this would be the price — the blood of four children barely older than his own. Was it really his fault? The irony of the question was nearly more than he could take, but whatever the answer, he also knew there was no turning back. He was the personification of the movement by now. A few weeks earlier, in the most triumphant moment of his life, he had spoken to a remarkable march on Washington, delivering the most powerful address that many of the people in the crowd had ever heard. It didn't start out that way. He was plodding at first through the printed text, almost reading, when he got caught up in the excitement of the day. The crowd was huge, maybe 200,000 people, a fourth of them white, spreading out from the base of the Lincoln Memorial. As he moved through the text, gazing out across the mass of jubilant faces, he remembered a passage he hadn't thought to include. He had used it before, and it had gone over well in Birmingham and Detroit, "and I just felt," he said much later, "that I wanted to use it here." So he pushed his printed text aside, and simply let the words pour out in a rush:

I say to you today, my friends, even though
we face the difficulties of today and tomorrow,

> I still have a dream. It is a dream deeply rooted
> in the American dream. I have a dream that
> one day this nation will rise up and live out the
> true meaning of its creed — we hold these
> truths to be self-evident, that all men are
> created equal.
>
> I have a dream that one day on the red hills
> of Georgia, the sons of former slaves and the
> sons of former slave-owners will be able to sit
> down together at the table of brotherhood.... I
> have a dream today!

It was a vision that became his gift to the country, an antidote to the tragedies of Birmingham and other places. And for some of us growing up in those times, it became an image that we couldn't put aside.

For me, however, the final conversion on the issue of race – the moment at which there was no going back — did not come until the following year, when I left Mobile and went away to the campus of Vanderbilt University. For many who came from other parts of the country, Vanderbilt was a stodgy and conservative place, a tree-shaded retreat on the western border of Nashville, where the sons and daughters of the American rich set out to test their academic mettle. The student body was overwhelmingly white, and in fact until the day that my class arrived, there had never been a black undergraduate at the school.

The first group was impressive — earnest and

bright — and I found it hard to explain to the student down the hall, making A's in calculus while I was fervently praying for a D, why his race was inherently inferior to mine. As basic as it sounds, it reinforced a sort of free-floating notion in my mind that I might have been raised on some faulty assumptions. But the moment of truth came later in the year, when George Wallace was invited to speak at Vanderbilt.

In the autumn of 1964, the governor of Alabama had made a run for the presidency, and even though he lost, the people back home were proud of his spunk. He had the pugnacious aura of a boxer (which he had been in his youth), though he had built his curious career on losing. In perhaps his most publicized act as governor, he stood in the doorway of the University of Alabama to block the admission of two black students, knowing full-well that they would be admitted anyway. Through-out those early years of his career, he became a lightning rod for the civil rights movement, almost assuring the kinds of changes he decried. But somehow it all played well in Alabama, a state still seething with lost-cause memories — the after shock of the great Civil War. It was a feeling that Wallace understood how to tap, and his popularity back home was astounding, even among people who should have known better.

There was a theory circulating among the Gaillards and others that the governor was really a moderate on race, making a principled stand on the issue of states rights. It was a theory that I badly wanted to accept — a gesture of loyalty, I suppose, to the family — but I was assigned during Wallace's visit to Vanderbilt to serve as one of his student hosts. We were standing backstage before the speech as the crowd began to gather at the gym: more than 3,000 people who were curious about him, with a few admirers and some others who had come to get a look at the devil.

"Do you think there'll be any niggers out there?"

The voice belonged unmistakably to Wallace, and the question was so bald and crude and startling that it took a moment to realize it was directed at me. I don't remember what I said, something about the speech being open to anyone, but Wallace merely shrugged and headed for the stage.

The ugly part came a few minutes later. There were, in fact, a few blacks in the crowd — a handful of students from Fisk University, well-mannered and brave, who had made the trip across town to ask him some questions. One girl rose with a trembling voice, and Wallace interrupted her question in the middle.

"What's that, honey? You'll have to speak up."

She tried again, and Wallace again cut her off with a sneer: "You're mighty pretty, honey. Go ahead with your question."

Many years later, George Wallace would change. Long after the murder of Martin Luther

King, after he, too, had been crippled by a would-be assassin, Wallace paid a visit to King's church in Montgomery. It was a remarkable moment in the little brick chapel, barely a block from the Alabama state capitol, where Jefferson Davis had taken his oath and "Dixie" had been chosen as the battle anthem of the South. Wallace, still governor but confined to a wheelchair, spoke of the redemptive power of suffering and the ability of God to change a man's heart — and as he was wheeled down the aisle at the end of the sermon, the congregation wept, and a hundred black hands reached out to touch him.

But all of that was well-hidden in the future. At Vanderbilt in 1965, the only thing we could feel, my friends from Alabama and I, was a deep sense of shame that this man was one of us. The alienation was stark, and over the next several months, we found ourselves searching for a new set of heroes. Actually, we didn't have far to look. Martin Luther King was one possibility. He was the winner of the Nobel Prize by now, and the following year, when he also paid a visit to the campus, he seemed to be everything Wallace was not. He was gentle and gracious and patient with those who didn't agree. But there was a figure who stirred us even more than King, and the reason, I think, had to do with his race. Robert Kennedy was white, and in the 1960s that was critically important.

If black Americans such as King were posing the questions, the great moral issues that the country had to face, it was up to the rest of us to decide how to answer. That, at least, was how it seemed at the time, and Kennedy was clearly a man who was trying. But perhaps it was even more basic than that. Perhaps I simply needed a white man to admire, and for an Alabama boy in the 1960s, the number of choices at the moment seemed small.

Whatever it was, Kennedy soon captivated our attention. He came to Vanderbilt in 1968, five days after he declared for the presidency. It was a chilly March night with a misting rain that would soon turn to ice, but nearly 11,000 people turned out to hear him, and there were that many more waiting for him at the airport. His plane was late, but the crowd simply grew, surging forward as soon as he appeared — screaming, waving signs, reaching out to shake his hand or just touch him. The intensity of it was almost frightening, but Kennedy smiled and climbed unsteadily to an escalator railing, where he made a brief speech about the problems of the country. The electricity of it was hard to define, but somewhere imbedded in his Massachusetts twang, in the jab of his forefinger and the tousle of his hair, in the enigmatic intensity of his icy blue stare, there was an urgency that was reflected and magnified in the crowd. For this was 1968, when the country seemed to be flying apart. In our history, of course, we had seen it before —

in the Civil War, certainly, and even at our founding, when the colonists had to choose between
competing imperatives: liberty on the one hand or
loyalty to the king. But the deepening divisions of
the 1960s — over poverty and race and the esca-
lating war in Vietnam — seemed so foreign to our
recent experience. World War II had brought us
together. We had responded as one when the
country was attacked, taking our stand against the
evils of Hitler, and in the course of those wrenching years of adventure, we had seen ourselves as
both righteous and strong. Now it was different.
Now our failures seemed to be laid bare, and some
people wondered how the country would survive.
Robert Kennedy, however, did not. He believed
that the strengths of the nation ran deep, and
because of that, he saw no need to gloss over its
problems.

In Kennedy's mind, those problems were serious — not only the war, but the pain he saw among
the country's have-nots. Kennedy identified with
that pain, and according to some of the people who
knew him, the empathy was rooted in the death of
his brother. Before that terrible morning in Dallas,
he seemed to be the consummate political opera-
tive, cynical and ruthless, a man who would do
nearly anything for his family. And even in 1968,
some people said he could still be ruthless, or at
least so driven that you couldn't tell the difference.
But he was not cynical. I remember the car ride

from the airport to Vanderbilt. Three local politicians had squeezed into the front seat, while Kennedy shared the back with the former astronaut, John Glenn, and me. I had been assigned to introduce him that night, and I rode along in astonished silence, while the politicians tried to tell him what to say. This is a campus audience, they said, so talk about Vietnam if you want. But it's also the South, so go a little easy on the subject of race.

Kennedy merely shrugged and rejected their advice. At Vanderbilt and every other stop on his campaign tour, he spoke with passion about the wounds in the country — "the violence," he said, "that afflicts the poor...the slow destruction of a child by hunger, and schools without books, and homes without any heat in the winter...."

But despite his pleadings, the wounds grew worse. On April 4, 1968, Martin Luther King was murdered in Memphis. Kennedy heard the news on a plane to Indianapolis, where he was scheduled to appear that night at a campaign rally in a black neighborhood. All across the country the ghettos were burning, with looting and bombs and sniper fire from the high-rise apartments. But Kennedy insisted on keeping his appointment. Standing alone on a flatbed truck, hunched against the cold in his black overcoat, he told the crowd what had happened to King, and as the people cried out in disbelief, he told them he understood how they felt.

"In this difficult day," he said, "in this difficult time for the United States, it is perhaps well to ask what kind of nation we are and what direction we want to move in. For those of you who are black...you can be filled with bitterness, with hatred, and a desire for revenge. We can move in that direction as a country, in great polarization — black people amongst black, white people amongst white, filled with hatred toward one another.

"Or we can make an effort, as Martin Luther King did, to understand and to comprehend, and to replace that violence, that stain of bloodshed that has spread across our land, with an effort to understand....

"My favorite poet was Aeschylus. He wrote: 'In our sleep, pain which cannot forget falls drop by drop upon the heart until, in our own despair, against our will, comes wisdom through the awful grace of God.'"

There were no riots in Indianapolis that night. "I guess the thing that kept us going," said one of King's aides, "was that maybe Bobby Kennedy would come up with some answers."

For the next two months, a lot of people held grimly to that hope, especially as Kennedy did well in the primaries, and the thought began slowly to form in our minds that despite all the tragedy and despair of the decade — the war and the riots and the murder of good men — Kennedy might really be the country's next president.

And then he was gone, following unbelievably in the martyred path of Dr. King. In a way, it was a culmination of the '60s, the death of the promise that had been so strong. There was nobody now to give it a voice — unless, one day, we could find it in ourselves.

During all of this time, visits home to Alabama were awkward at best. In retrospect, it was partly my fault, for I was a convert now, a lover of the truth, eager to enlighten the people left behind. I remember one particular night in Mobile when I was lecturing the family on the latest outrage. There had been a killing up the road in Lowndes County. A civil rights worker named Jonathan Daniel, a white Episcopal priest from Massachusetts, was murdered in the sleepy little town of Hayneville — shot down in front of a group of eyewitnesses, all of them black, by a prominent white man who lived in the area. The killer's lawyer made a simple defense, arguing not that his client was innocent, but that Jonathan Daniel — a "white nigger" from the North, as they said in Alabama — had gotten pretty much what he deserved. An all-white jury let the killer go free.

I was home on break, and I told some family members at the house that it made me ashamed to be from the state. I was sitting, as I spoke, in a small rocking chair, lounging back comfortably, when an uncle from my mother's side of the family suddenly decided that he had heard enough. He bolted angrily across the room, and with both hands braced on the arms of my chair — his face only a couple of inches from mine — he called me a traitor to my family and the South. Not to be outdone, I called him a race-baiting son of a bitch, then pushed him aside and stalked from the house.

For me at least, it was a moment of hurt. I was fond of my uncle and knew him as a good and decent man. He was a courageous veteran of World War II, having survived the fighting in the Ardennes Forest — the Battle of the Bulge, the Americans called it, when the German army rallied for one last assault. It was December of 1944, six months after D-Day, and everybody knew that Hitler had lost. But the Fueher himself was not yet convinced, and when he threw everything he had at the Luxembourg border, he created at first a 60-mile bulge in the American lines. For awhile, the fighting was nearly hand-to-hand, as confusion reigned in the evergreen forests, but after six weeks the Americans had won, and Germans by the thousands lay dead in the snow.

My uncle never talked about it much, though he brooded sometimes as he puttered around his farm in Montgomery County. It was a place he owned with his father and his brother — 2,000 acres of black-dirt prairie, rolling eastward from the Lowndes County line. White-faced cattle grazed on the hills, and stands of pine soon gave way to black-water swamps. As a boy, I roamed every inch of the place, learning to ride with the help of old Mack, a swaybacked bay nearly 30 years old. He was an animal wise in the ways of young children, gentle and sure, not much given to stubbornness or fright. We scouted the range for renegades and outlaws, until one fine day on the strength of his teaching, our cowboy games gave way to the real thing. The work was hard — long days in the sun chasing steers or cutting hay, sometimes castrating the newborn calves, but all in all it was a satisfying place for a boy to spend the summer.

Life, however, was a little more grim for some of the others on the same piece of land. The farm in the 1950s and '60s was worked in part by a group of blacks who lived in small and unpainted cabins without electricity or indoor plumbing. A few of them turned their jobs into art — cooking, training horses, performing with consummate pride and skill all the functions that were necessary to the farm. Others, however, merely tried to get by, putting in their time until nightfall finally brought a reprieve. Those of us not a part of that life never knew very much about the nights — what mysteries lay concealed in the black peoples' cabins — though a small boy could lie in his bed and wonder.

That was particularly true on the night Savannah came screaming to the house. "Mr. Ned!" she cried, "Mr. Ned, Mr. Ned! You gotta help me, Mr. Ned. The man's gonna kill me!" Savannah was a cook who worked at the farm, and she was fighting that night with a man at her cabin. We never knew why. An infidelity perhaps? Attention withheld? Those were some of the points of speculation, but whatever the case, Savannah was drunk and afraid for her life, and she had fled across the fields to the only haven she knew.

"I'm staying here with my white folks!" she screamed.

Out in the car, the man yelled back, threatening more harm if she didn't come out. My uncle surveyed the whole scene calmly, then shook his head and strolled toward the car.

"We don't need any trouble," he announced. "You better move on." And he knew when he said it that the man would obey.

My uncle's conception of the issue of race was shaped, of course, by moments such as that, while mine was shaped by Martin Luther King. The chasm between us should have come as no surprise.

Somewhere near the height of my estrangement from the family, when it seemed most permanent and impossible to bridge, I received a telephone call from Mobile, bringing the news that my father was sick. There had been a hemorrhage somewhere in his brain, and he had been in convulsions for more than a day. The doctors weren't sure if he would make it or not.

I rushed home as quickly as I could get there and was startled by the scene in intensive care. My father lay on the bed, a bloody gauze turban wrapped around his head and his mind roaming free. "I died last night," he told me with a sob. It was a staggering transformation of a man who, only a few days before, had been at his office in the Mobile courthouse. Walter Gaillard was a circuit judge, one step below the Alabama Supreme Court, and there were some who said he could have risen even higher. But he was not particularly ambitious that way. His prayer every day was for wisdom and justice and the ability to make his own father proud.

He struggled sometimes with Palmer Gaillard's shadow, wondering inexplicably if his own generation would ever measure up. His work was his justification and his proof, a bastion of meaning he had found for his life, and suddenly with his stroke it was taken away. For nearly five years, he battled to recover, but in the end the damage was simply too severe. I came home to see him in the last few weeks, bringing my wife who was four months pregnant. He was in and out of a coma by now, but in one of those moments when his mind was lucid, he put his hand on her stomach and waited for the kick. "Cycle of life," he whispered when it came, and I thought I saw the faintest tremor of a smile as he slipped back into unconsciousness again.

Within a few more days he was gone.

I found myself thinking about the family after that — about a legacy that was rich and complicated and strong. For generations, going back all the way to colonial times, there had been a deep attachment to the status quo — a reluctance to embrace the American Revolution, or to confront the implications of slavery and segregation. To a person coming of age in the 1960s, it was hard to identify proudly with that. And yet there was something that I felt a part of, something that I couldn't shake loose from my mind, even if it took me many years to define it.

I don't suppose the definition was complete until the day in 1993, when I was going once again through my grandfather's attic. The Big House was standing empty by then, soon to be rented out, the last relatives gone. I was sorting my way through the centuries of clutter, when I came across the letters of Thomas Gaillard and the sketch that he had written about his father, Captain Peter. Struck by the startling familiarity of the voices, I thought about something my grandfather had said. We had gathered one night for the reading of the Bible — my aunts and my father and the old man and me, and before he began, he patted my shoulder with his frail, bony hand. "This boy will surpass me," he announced to the others.

I was barely 12 years old at the time, but my

relatives reacted with appropriate solemnity, as if he had detected in his youngest grandson some hidden spark, some flicker of genius, that would carry the family name to new heights. But it seemed to me that it was a different kind of prophecy. Not that I gave it much thought at the time, but later in the stillness of the old man's attic, I knew he was thinking of the generations before us: the gift of Captain Peter, whose gratitude saved him from the sins of the rich; and the integrity of Thomas, as his fortunes declined and the country around him descended into war. In my grandfather's case, there was a history of kindness and a deep, private struggle with the issue of justice.

I think he knew in the final years of his life that we were living on the edge of a monumental change — something in the realm of the emigration from France, or the revolution that led to the founding of the country. But whatever was coming, it was the duty of the next generation to live it – to add what we could to the legacy of the ancestors. Looking back on it now, the only surprise was that it came so easy. I don't mean to say that the country didn't suffer a terrible price, or that there wasn't some baggage that had to be shed. But at least for some of us raised in the South, there were pieces of wisdom that served us very well.

In those last, troubled days of segregation, many of us seemed to be rejecting the past, and may even have thought of it that way in our minds.

135

In fact, however, we were seeking to expand it —
to apply the color-blind principles of civility and
respect to the problem of two races living side by
side.

The transformation is far from complete, with
the resurgence of prejudice, the rising crime rate in
black neighborhoods and the dangers of poverty
and alienation and violence. But there is value
even now in listening to the elders, in sifting
through the lessons that have been handed down
— seeking out the traces of wisdom that survive.

Notes and
Acknowledgements

This book is intended purely as a work of non-fiction. No characters have been invented, no dialogue contrived, and whenever the historical record was bare, I left it that way.

The fact that the story can be told at all is a tribute to the genealogists in the family and the people through the years who have preserved old letters and records of the past. Among those still living, I would like to thank my cousins Robert Palmer, Palmer Hamilton, Tommy Gaillard and G. Rayner Gaillard. My grandfather, Palmer Gaillard, and his daughters, Mary and Flora Gaillard, were also faithful keepers of the record, storing in their attic many boxloads of old papers and relics. They also updated a genealogy prepared by Palmer Gaillard's aunt, Marianne Gaillard Spratley. That genealogy, in turn, was based on work by Thomas Gaillard (Marianne Spratley's father) and a cousin, William D. Gaillard of New York. The most complete *Gaillard Genealogy*, covering all branches of the family descended from the immigrants in South Carolina, was prepared by Dorothy Kelly MacDowell of Aiken, S.C. Other helpful writings by members of the family included *The River Plantation* by Caroline Gaillard Hurtel and *Plantations of the Carolina Low Country* by Samuel Gaillard Stoney.

Thomas Gaillard, my great-great-grandfather and an important character in this narrative, wrote informative contemporary sketches of many members of the family, and of the areas of South Carolina and Alabama where he lived. His work was made available to me by my cousin, Palmer Hamilton of Mobile. Also included in the Hamilton papers, as well as those of my grandfather, were contemporary sketches and anecdotes from the Low Country by social historians Samuel DuBose and Frederick Porcher. In addition, Mrs. Leize Gaillard left behind a brief sketch of the Rocks, the South Carolina planatation home of my great-great-great-grandfather, Capt. Peter Gaillard. Peter himself left detailed plantation records, which have been studied perceptively by a number of historians, especially Cheryll Ann Cody of the University of Minnesota. Her article, "Naming,

Kinship, and Estate Dispersal: Notes on Slave Family Life on a South Carolina Plantation, 1786 to 1833," was published by the *William and Mary Quarterly*, January 1982.

In my own work, I have relied on these sources in addition to old letters and other documents found at the South Carolina Historical Society, the Southern historical collection at the University of North Carolina library, the Alabama Archives and the collections preserved by members of my family. I have endeavored to piece the story together and then to place it in historical context, which required, in effect, a crash diet of reading on the history of the South. I was guided in my choice of material by some fading recollections from my days as a history major at Vanderbilt, and by consultations with a handful of excellent historians, including David Goldfield, Dan Dupre and Dan Morrill of the University of North Carolina at Charlotte; Robert Whalen of Queens College, and John Rogers of Charlotte.

With their guidance, I relied on the following books, among others: *South Carolina: a Synoptic History for Laymen*, by Lewis P. Jones; *The Southern Frontier*, by Verner W. Crane; *Lawson's History of North Carolina*, by John Lawson; *Charleston in the Age of the Pinckneys*, by George C. Rogers Jr.; *South Carolina Loyalists in the American Revolution*, by Robert Stansbury Lambert; *Southern Campaigns of the American*

Revolution, by Dan L. Morrill; *Patriots: The Men Who Started the American Revolution*, by A.J. Langguth; *The Swamp Fox*, by Robert D. Bass; *The Life of Henry Laurens*, by David Duncan Wallace; *The American South: A History*, by William J. Cooper, Jr. and Thomas E. Terrill; *A Rage for Order*, by Joel Williamson; *Ar'n't I a Woman: Female Slaves In The Plantation South*, by Deborah Gray White; *Plantations of the Low Country: South Carolina 1697-1865*, photograpy by N. Jane Isley, written and researched by William P. Baldwin and Agnes L. Baldwin; *A Family Venture: Men and Women On The Southern Frontier*, by Joan E. Cashin; *The Politics of Indian Removal*, by Michael D. Green; *Andrew Jackson and the Creek War*, by James W. Holland; *McIntosh and Weatherford, Creek Indian Leaders*, by Benjamin W. Griffith, Jr.; *The Civil War*, a narrative trilogy by Shelby Foote; *Reconstruction: America's Unfinished Revolution*, by Eric Foner; *Black, White and Southern*, by David R. Goldfield; *Augusta Evans Wilson: A Biography*, by William Perry Fidler; *Mobile in the 1850s: A Social, Cultural and Economic History*, by Robert L. Robinson; *The Great War in Modern Memory*, by Paul Fussell; *A Short History of World War II*, by James L. Stokesbury; *Bearing The Cross: Martin Luther King, Jr., And The Southern Christian Leadership Conference*, by David Garrow; *Let The Trumpet Sound: The Life of Martin Luther King,*

Jr., by Stephen B. Oates; *Leaving Birmingham: Notes of a Native Son*, by Paul Hemphill; and *RFK: Collected Speeches*, edited and introduced by Edwin O. Guthman and C. Richard Allen.

My debt to all of these authors is detailed in the notes that follow. I want to make it clear, however, that for better or worse the overall interpretations in this book are mine — a synthesis of information from primary sources, copies of family papers handed down through the years, bits of oral history here and there and works of scholarship by many different writers.

With all of those sources supplying the facts, I have tried to fashion a coherent story. This book is the truth as I understand it.

Notes By Chapter

Chapter 1 — The information on the Gaillards in France comes from the genealogy my grandfather prepared, a small book simply entitled *Gaillard*. The story of a cousin who was tortured on the rack was documented in that genealogy and also passed on as a piece of oral history all the way to my aunt, Mary Gaillard, who told it with great indignation and flourish.

The account of the hurricane of 1686 and the descriptions of Charleston in its earliest days come from *South Carolina: A Synoptic History for Laymen*, by Lewis P. Jones. Additional information comes from George Rogers' *Charleston in the Age of the Pinckneys*. A copy of the original land grant to the immigrant, Joachim Gaillard, appears in Dorothy Kelly MacDowell's *Gaillard Genealogy*.

The story of the explorer John Lawson's visit to the Gaillards in 1701 is taken from Lawson's own journal, but also is mentioned in MacDowell's genealogy and in articles by several historians of the period. Lawson mentions no first names (in fact, he misspells Gaillard), and there has been some dispute about exactly which members of the family he visited. Most accounts agree on Bartholomew, Joachim Gaillard's most prominent son, and it seems likely that Lawson met Joachim himself, since he refers to Mons. Gaillard, "the elder." Joachim, at the time, would have been 75, while his sons would still have been in their 30s.

The records of Bartholomew's prominence in the early affairs of his colony are contained in MacDowell's genealogy. My grandfather's book reports that Bartholomew "saw service in the Indian wars of that period." The account of those wars and the relationship between the Indians and the settlers is pieced together from Verner Crane's *The Southern Frontier* and the Lewis Jones history of South Carolina. The account of an Indian raid on the plantation of Theodore Gaillard is taken from a letter written by his fellow colonist, John

Gendron, on September 24, 1751, and reprinted in MacDowell's genealogy.

Theodore's purchase of land from his sister, after inheriting the shares of his late older brother, is recorded in the probate court records of the colony and reprinted in MacDowell's genealogy. The struggles of the early planters to cultivate rice, and then indigo, are described in Jones' history of South Carolina, Rogers' history of Charleston in the time of the Pinckneys and in the history textbook, *The American South*, by William J. Cooper and Thomas Terrill.

Cooper and Terrill write with great clarity about the idea of liberty and its power among the colonists in the years just before the American Revolution. My grandfather's genealogy offers a glimpse of the anguish of the early Gaillards as they were caught between the pull of liberty on the one hand and loyalty to the king. David Duncan Wallace's biography of Henry Laurens makes it clear that they were not alone. Wallace, along with Lewis P. Jones, also provides a thorough account of the Provincial Congresses just before the revolution, attended by at least three of the Gaillards.

The conflict between the ideal of liberty and the institution of slavery is described by Cooper and Terrill, and the ugly fratricide of the Revolutionary era is recorded in a number of places, including Dan Morrill's *Southern Campaigns of the American Revolution*. The story of the flogging of an old Tory by a renegade member of Francis Marion's brigade is described in Robert Bass's biography, *The Swamp Fox*. The story of the aging patriot, John Palmer, being locked in a burial vault is told by a contemporary, Samuel DuBose, in his "Reminiscences of St. Stephens Parish, Craven County, South Carolina," an essay handed down in the papers of my grandfather and my cousin, Palmer Hamilton.

The story of Tacitus Gaillard and his ironic flight to Louisiana is told in abbreviated form in my grandfather's genealogy, and at greater length in an article by Susan Smythe Bennett in the *Transactions of the Hugenot Society of South Carolina, #38* (1933). The Bennett article is excerpted in the MacDowell genealogy.

Chapter 2 — The account of Peter Gaillard's early life is taken from the text of a speech by Samuel DuBose, delivered on April 27, 1858. Samuel's father, also named Samuel DuBose, was one of Peter Gaillard's closest friends. Peter's difficulty in picking sides in the war is recorded in that same speech by DuBose, and in an essay by Peter's grandson, Richebourg Gaillard. Copies of those papers were preserved by my grandfather, as well as in the papers of Palmer Hamilton.

The loyalist sympathies of Peter's father, Theodore Gaillard, are acknowledged in my grandfather's genealogy and in the DuBose papers. The activites of Peter's older brothers, John and Theodore Jr., in support of the king are detailed in the book, *South Carolina Loyalists in the American Revolution*, by Robert S. Lambert.

Accounts of the major battles of the Revolution — Charleston, Savannah, Kings Mountain and Yorktown — as well as the strategies of Nathaniel Greene are taken primarily from Dan Morrill's *Southern Campaigns of the American Revolution*.

The description of Peter Gaillard as he went off to war is pieced together from a contemporary account by Frederick Porcher in his "Historical and Social Sketches of Craven County, South Carolina," and oral history accounts handed down by my grandfather and my aunt, Mary Gaillard. The account of the Battle of Black Mingo, Peter's first taste of bloodshed, is taken from The Swamp Fox by Robert Bass, and from the contemporary account of Samuel DuBose.

Peter Gaillard's decision to change sides in the war, and his welcome into the ranks of his neighbor, Francis Marion, are recorded by DuBose (whose father was the go-between in the switch) and by Peter's grandson, Richebourg Gaillard. It is mentioned in other family papers, including, ironically, the D.A.R. application of my aunt, Mary Gaillard. The horse that Marion rode on that occasion is described in *The Swamp Fox*. The description of Marion is taken from his portraits.

145

The salutes exchanged by Marion and Peter are part of the oral history handed down in the family. The account of the battle around Biggin Church is pieced together from compatible versions in *The Swamp Fox* and in the DuBose papers. The story of the death of John Laurens in Peter Gaillard's last battle is taken from DuBose and from a detailed account in *The Life of Henry Laurens* by David Duncan Wallace.

Chapter 3 — Samuel DuBose provides the account of the suspicion and hostility Peter Gaillard encountered from some of his neighbors, who regarded him as Benedict Arnold in reverse. The trial of John Gaillard is described in *South Carolina Loyalists in the American Revolution*. Peter's economic struggles are chronicled in accounts by DuBose, Frederick Porcher and his son, Thomas Gaillard. More general accounts of the post-war economy in South Carolina were taken from Lewis Jones' history and from *The American South* by Cooper and Terrill.

Peter's extraordinary good fortune in winning a lottery to stave off ruin was chronicled by his son, Thomas, and in the book, *Plantations of the Low Country*, by Iseley and Baldwin. His pioneering of cotton in his corner of the Low Country is reported by DuBose and Porcher, and DuBose records Peter's use of the cotton gin in 1796, only three years after its invention by Eli Whitney. The story of that invention is taken from the *World Book Encyclopedia*.

The building of the Rocks, Peter's new home in South Carolina, is recorded in his own plantation notebook, and excerpted in *Plantations of the Low Country*. His skill as a wood-carver is described by his contemporary, Frederick Porcher, in Porcher's "Historical and Social Sketch of Craven County, South Carolina."

The section of this chapter dealing with slavery is pieced together from Lewis Jones' history of South Carolina, Cooper and Terrill's history of the South, David Wallace's biography of Henry Laurens, historian Joel Williamson's outstanding study of race relations, *A Rage for Order*, and Cheryll Ann Cody's even-handed study of Peter Gaillard's plantation records. Peter's great-grandson, Palmer Gaillard (my grandfather), affirms the family's article of faith that Peter was extraordinarily kind to his slaves.

Peter's plantation notebook is preserved on microfilm in several locations, including the Charlotte-Mecklenburg public library, and it was there that I read it, noting not only the content, but the elegant, looping style of the script. His initial depression at giving up the plantation life due to the mounting infirmities of old age is recorded by his son, Thomas. His final letter to the members of his family is quoted in full in the genealogy prepared by Palmer Gaillard.

Chapter 4 — Thomas Gaillard's childhood is described in his own memoir, handed down in my grandfather's papers and in the papers preserved by Palmer Hamilton. The description of his abilities and style as a speaker is taken from notes by his son, Richebourg Gaillard, also preserved in the same sets of papers. In addition, Thomas offers a detailed and startlingly candid description of his financial struggles and his career as a politician, including his lopsided defeat when he ran for the legislature in 1830.

The account of the nullification controversy of 1828 is put together from Cooper and Terrill's history of the South, Lewis Jones' history of South Carolina, encyclopedia descriptions of the life of John C. Calhoun and Thomas Gaillard's recollections. The descriptions of the slave rebellions led by Nat Turner and Denmark Vesey — and the subsequent hardening of Southern attitudes about slavery — are taken from Cooper and Terrill, Lewis Jones and Joel Williamson. The quote from Thomas Gaillard's wife, Marianne, is taken from a letter to her brother, John Palmer.

The ugly climate surrounding the election of 1830 is described by Lewis Jones, and Thomas' decision soon afterward to move to Alabama is chronicled in his own memoirs, as well as in writings by his son, Richebourg, and his grandson, Palmer Gaillard.

Chapter 5 — The story of the move to Alabama is taken from Caroline Gaillard Hurtel's *The River Plantation*, a biography of her great-grandfather, Thomas Gaillard. The account of the Indian wars in Alabama is pieced together from three narratives: *Andrew Jackson and the Creek War* by James W. Holland, *The Politics of Indian Removal* by Michael Green, and *McIntosh and Weatherford, Creek Indian Leaders* by Benjamin W. Griffith.

Thomas Gaillard's description of the frontier violence of Alabama is taken from a letter to his older brother, Peter Gaillard Jr., written on December 14, 1837. The loneliness and anguish of frontier women in the South is described in Joan Cashin's *A Family Venture*, and Marianne Gaillard's overpowering homesickness and worry about her family's financial problems after the move to Alabama are described in a string of letters in the 1840s, written to her brother, John Palmer. The letters were preserved by Robert Palmer, one of her descendants in South Carolina, who kindly made them available to me. Some of them also appear in Caroline Gaillard Hurtel's *The River Plantation*.

Thomas' book, *The History of the Reformation*, is still available in many libraries, including the Queens College library in Charlotte, N.C. In his memoirs handed down through the family, he describes the ordeal of writing it, along with two others in a trilogy about the church — the last of which he decided to burn.

His sons' adventure in the California gold rush is recounted in *The River Plantation*. The strange fatal illness of his oldest son John is taken from an essay by John's grandson, John Gaillard Hamilton, handed down in the papers of Palmer Hamilton. The death of Marianne is described in a poignant letter from Thomas to Marianne's brother, John Palmer, written on August 15, 1860.

The account of Thomas putting a row of candles in his window when Alabama seceded from the Union in January of 1861 is taken from *The River Plantation*. His mixed feelings about secession are recorded in my grandfather's genealogy. The overall backdrop of secession and war is based on the accounts of Cooper and Terrill and of Shelby Foote in *The Civil War*. Franklin Gaillard's account of the Battle of Bull Run was contained in a letter to his father, written on August 4, 1861. Franklin's letters from the war, striking in their eloquence, were gathered and bound by members of his family and can be found in the rare books collection at the University of North Carolina library and at the South Carolina Historical Society in Charleston.

Thomas' gloom about the war was expressed in letters written to his children in April and July of 1862. Those letters are now in the good hands of my cousin, Tommy Gaillard, of Jackson, Ala. In addition, Thomas' son Richebourg, in an essay in memory of his father, recorded Thomas' early and accurate predictions of the Confederate defeat. The accounts of the wartime experiences of Thomas' other sons, Edmund, Samuel and Richebourg, are taken from *The River Plantation*, and from an undated letter that Richebourg wrote from Camp Chase, Ohio, after he was taken prisoner.

The vivid description of the field hospitals, where Edmund and Samuel both served in the war, is taken from Cooper and Terrill's *The American South*.

Chapter 6 — The description of the final battles and strategy of the Civil War, including the Battle of the Wilderness where Franklin Gaillard was killed, is pieced together from Shelby Foote's *The Civil War*, and from Cooper and Terrill. The death of Franklin is described in *The River Plantation*, which also contains an account of the prison camp experiences of Samuel Gaillard after he was captured and sent to Ship Island off the Mississippi coast. My grandfather's genealogy also records those experiences, including the fact that Samuel suffered "cruelty and humiliation ... at the hands of colored troops."

The Gaillards' hatred of Thaddeus Stevens during the Reconstruction era is described with lingering bitterness in my grandfather's book. The overall descriptions of Reconstruction are taken primarily from Eric Foner's epic work on the subject, as well as Joel Williamson's *A Rage for Order* and the Southern history text of Cooper and Terrill. The account of the economic plight of the Gaillards, and the decision of Caroline Gaillard not to sell her slaves as the Civil War was approaching an end, are taken from *The River Plantation* and from conversations with my grandfather.

The descriptions of the appalling racial violence at the end of Reconstruction are taken primarily from the works of Williamson and Foner. The accounts of the restoration of the Gaillard family come from my grandfather. The rather startling quote about the superiority of the white race is his also, taken from an article he wrote for the *Journal of the Alabama Bar Association*.

Chapter 7 — The description of the relationship between my grandfather and his wife-to-be, Maddie Wilson, is taken from the letters he wrote to her while she was studying music in New York. I found the letters in my grandfather's attic. Maddie's letters of reply apparently did not survive, but in many cases the content is easily inferred from my grandfather's answers.

The description of Ashland Place, the estate of Maddie's family, is taken from William Perry Fidler's biography, *Augusta Evans Wilson*, and from my grandfather's book of genealogy. The account of the killing of Maddie's father is taken from Fidler —and from the indignant notes that my aunt, Mary Gaillard, wrote in the margins of his book. It was also a story told often in the family.

The description of the estate that Palmer Gaillard bought for Maddie after they were married is contained in his genealogy, and it is the place, of course, where I spent a great deal of my childhood. The account of the ravages of yellow fever in Mobile is based on Robert L. Robinson's social and cultural history of the city. My grandfather's stoic account of the death of his wife was written on an envelope that I found in his attic.

Woodrow Wilson's visit to Mobile was recorded in the *Mobile Press Register*. I found my grandfather's invitation to the event in his attic. Wilson's White House showing of "The Birth of a Nation" is described in Joel Williamson's *A Rage for Order*. The general descriptions of World War I are based primarily on Paul Fussell's *The Great War in Modern Memory*. The wartime experiences of Palmer Gaillard Jr. are taken partly from his letters, now in the possession of his daughter, Julie Suk, and partly from the accounts of his brother, Wilson Gaillard, written in a small book, *Strangest Story I've Ever Heard*.

In his genealogy, my grandfather describes his years as the lawyer for Mobile's congressman, Frank Boykin, including his final case, which he argued at the age of 97 before the Alabama supreme court. Their relationship also is described in a testimonial by Boykin in the *Congressional Record*, June 21, 1957.

The story of my aunts, Mary and Flora Gaillard, is taken from my own recollections and those of my cousin, Julie Suk, who spent many hours at the Big House as well and read Flora's letters shortly after her death. The quote from one of Flora's suitors is taken from a close paraphrase in a poem by Julie Suk — one of the best in her volume, *The Angel of Obsession*, published by the University of Arkansas Press. The backdrop of desegregation in Little Rock is taken in part from David Goldfield's *Black, White and Southern*. Flora's vow to isolate any black child assigned to her class was something I heard her say on several occasions.

The description of Mary Gaillard's story-telling gift is based, of course, on my own experience. The relationship between Robert Croshon and my grandfather was described by Robert in an interview in the summer of 1987, which led to an article in the *Charlotte Observer*, published June 28. The story of the flight from slavery by Robert's ancestors was told by Robert, and also by his brother, Edward Croshon, who, among his other activities, has become a dedicated social historian of Mobile.

My grandfather's role in his church was described by his minister, John Crowell, in an interview on April 5, 1994. Dr. Crowell also provided me with several letters that my grandfather had written to the elders. The description of my grandfather on his deathbed is taken in part from my own memory. His final conversation with John Crowell was recounted, of course, by Dr. Crowell.

Chapter 8 — The recollections of my relationship with Robert Croshon, and through him, my first encounter with the practice of segregation, are my own. Most of this chapter falls into that category — my memories of Bear Bryant, my encounter with George Wallace at Vanderbilt, with Martin Luther King in Birmingham and Robert Kennedy in Nashville; my recollections of the family farm in Montgomery, my painful disagreement with one of my uncles, my memories of my father at the end of his life. All of these remain vivid in my mind.

The story of Martin Luther King's first speech during the Montgomery bus boycott is taken primarily from Stephen B. Oates' biography, *Let The Trumpet Sound.* My summary of the civil rights struggle in Birmingham is based on David Garrow's *Bearing The Cross,* Paul Hemphill's *Leaving Birmingham,* as well as interviews that I did with participants in the struggle. (Those interviews led to a lengthy piece on King that appears in an earlier book, *Southern Voices.*) The story of the "I Have A Dream" speech comes from David Garrow.

I was a witness to George Wallace's crude

comments backstage at Vanderbilt, and also from the podium. The quotes are taken from my memory. Wallace's poignant visit years later to the church of Martin Luther King was described in an article by one of Alabama's great journalists, Ray Jenkins, and in David Goldfield's book, *Black, White and Southern*. The account of Robert Kennedy's visit to Vanderbilt is taken from my memory, and from the book *RFK: Collected Speeches*. His speech after the murder of Martin Luther King also is taken from that collection.

The brief description of the Battle of the Bulge, where my uncle served bravely in World War II, is taken from James L. Stokesbury's *A Short History of World War II*. My final thoughts on the family appeared in different form in the book, *Southern Voices*.

I am grateful to my wife, Nancy Gaillard, who helped in the research for this book, and to my daughters, Rachel and Tracy Gaillard, who inspired it and offered encouragement along the way. I also am grateful to my editor and publisher, Jerry Bledsoe, who believed from the start that a project this deeply personal might hold an interest for somebody else.